ROYAL
RECIPES

✣ ✣

ROYAL RECIPES

MICHÈLE BROWN

PAVILION

New edition first published in Great Britain in 1995 by
Pavilion Books Limited
26 Upper Ground
London SE1 9PD

First published in 1977 by Elm Tree Books
The moral right of the author has been asserted

Text copyright © 1977 by Michèle Brown
Illustrations and jacket illustration © 1995 by John Lawrence

Designed by Nigel Partridge

A CIP catalogue record for this book is available from
the British Library

ISBN 1-85793-6914

Typeset in Caslon 540

Printed and bound in Great Britain by
Butler & Tanner Ltd, Frome and London

2 4 6 8 10 9 7 5 3 1

This book may be ordered by post direct from the publisher.
Please contact the Marketing Department.
But try your bookshop first.

CONTENTS

✣ ✣

✢ ✢

ꞤOTE ON THE ℳEASUREMENTS

Although ingredients have been listed with both metric and imperial measures, these are never exactly equivalent amounts and it is most important to follow one set or the other. 25 g to 500 ml provides the same solid/liquid ratio as 1 oz to 1 pint; if the metric measures are followed, the recipe will yield about 10 per cent less.

INTRODUCTION

✣ ✣

THIS BOOK is about the food eaten by the English kings and queens from William the Conqueror to Edward VII – a period covering nearly a thousand years. In 1066 William brought to this country the style of cooking which was then standard all over Western Europe. Edward VII brings us right up to the beginning of the twentieth century and it seems appropriate to leave the story of royal food with a king who was famous as a bon viveur and whose name has become synonymous with an elegant way of life now gone for good. Since Edward VII's time one gets the impression that the Royal Family have been eating much the same sort of fare as the rest of us, which may be highly commendable but is scarcely exciting.

The fact that our monarchs had a more interesting and more ostentatious diet than the majority of their people does not mean that their food is difficult to recreate today. When William the Conqueror came to the throne most people were on a subsistence level diet and ingredients counted as luxuries then – eggs, cream, chicken, spices and fresh fruit – are much more generally available now. What is more, kitchens were inefficient, using fires and eventually coal stoves, and had little labour-saving equipment. What was once only feasible for a royal kitchen with vast numbers of staff is now possible for anyone with an average labour-saving kitchen. The recipes in this book use ingredients which are readily obtainable in the shops, and require no special equipment. Although some of them have been slightly adapted to suit a modern kitchen they are all authentic and taken from recipe books of their period. I have been surprised at how well these old recipes work, and how delicious the results are, particularly when the original wording looks distinctly unpromising. The Old English sometimes makes a dish sound very unappetising indeed and the no-frills approach can be rather unnerving – 'Take a gurnard rawe, and slytte him endelonge the bak, through the head and tail, and splatte him and keep the liver ...' 'Take fleysshe of Capoun or of Porke, & hakke him smalle...' is the usual style. In these medieval recipes particularly, there is also a disregard for precise quantities and a tendency to mix apparently incompatible ingredients like fresh apples and bone marrow. This partly explains why they have been neglected for so long by practical cooks. Fortunately these very idiosyncrasies have made the ancient recipe books a constant source of delight to scholarly clerical gentlemen over the past two hundred years. I am deeply indebted to these Reverend gentlemen who, while they would not have dreamed of eating the food, have deciphered many of the early manuscripts and edited them so they are reasonably comprehensible.

From the seventeenth to the nineteenth century research into royal recipes becomes progressively easier, for Court Chefs began to cash in on their reputations by publishing their own recipe books. Joseph Cooper, Master Chef to Charles I, began it all with his book *The Art of Cookery Refined and Augmented*. Patrick Lambe, whose long career spanned the reigns of Charles II, James II, William and Mary, and Queen Anne, summed up his technique in *Royal Cookery or the Complete Court Cook* published in 1710. Carême, who for a short time was cook to George IV, wrote a number of books on French Cookery, and two of Queen Victoria's chefs, Soyer and Francatelli, were also prolific on the subject. *A Guide to Modern Cookery* by Escoffier, who cooked for Edward VII, is a culinary classic.

Naturally the nearer we get to our own century the more familiar the dishes and meals become. I am most grateful to family and friends who have eaten and enjoyed the different dishes that have been tried out (and would like to extend special thanks to Penelope Norris for her invaluable help with recipe-testing). Some, it must be admitted, have been conscientiously eaten but not enjoyed – these are not in the book. One or two curiosities, such as *Viper Soup*, have been discarded without further ado, but on the whole I have tried to keep an open mind about what to experiment with and I have been rewarded with some delicious results from recipes I have tried without much hope of success. One of my favourites is *Bor in Counfett* (p. 70) a fifteenth-century dish of cold pork served in a honey and wine sauce. Having tried a wide range of sweet and savoury dishes from all periods I am surprised at the poor reputation that English cooking has gained for itself. *Stewed Pigeon with Garlic*, *Salmon in Champagne*, *Darioles* and *Floating Islands* can hold their own against any continental dishes. The undoubted excellence of the French Master Chefs and the intricacies of their brand of *haute cuisine* have somehow led us to assume that because our cooking is different it is inferior, which is definitely untrue, especially where English home cooking is concerned.

In the sixteenth and seventeenth centuries we were considered very good cooks indeed and we were famous for our sweet and savoury pies. These used to be available in an infinite number of varieties, which seem to have dwindled to apple pie or steak and kidney pie. It is high time that the other traditional fillings like cherries cooked in mulled wine (p. 100) were rediscovered and appreciated.

Of course if you are taking the trouble to recreate a meal of a particular period it is nice to know that you are serving the correct drink as well. This is a comparatively simple matter, for the drinks of the past thousand years have not changed very much. Wine was always popular, especially sweet wine, as there seems to be no period when the English did not have a sweet tooth. This sweet wine was often imported from the Levant and a sweet white wine from Greece would be appropriate with food at any period until the mid-seventeenth century. Alternatively serve French Burgundy or the Rhenish wine from the Rhine region This type was particularly popular with the Tudors. Beer was always a favourite with rich and poor. Strictly speaking the 'Ale' which accompanies food up until the end of the fifteenth century should be brewed without hops, which were introduced from the Continent in the sixteenth century. One writer of the time, appalled at the new-fangled foreign habit of spoiling good English ale with hops wrote 'it is a naturall drynke for a Dutche man. And now of late days it is moch used in England, to *the detryment of many Englysshe men.*' Elizabeth I drank light, freshly brewed beer and took great exception at being offered strong ale.

After dinner a sweetened and spiced mulled wine called Hypocras was served at the Court and in very wealthy households as an aid to digestion. This was common practice until the middle of the seventeenth century when French influence, which became very strong with the return of Charles II from exile in France, saw the gradual introduction of brandy as the accepted after-dinner drink. Champagne was brought to this country at the same time but really came into its own as a status symbol about a hundred years later. The seventeenth century was also the period when the three non-alcoholic drinks we now take for granted – tea, coffee and chocolate – were introduced to Europe from the New World. All three were even more expensive three hundred years ago than they are now, but they immediately became popular for there was nothing else like them. These non-alcoholic beverages were considered very much as ladies' drinks and the Queens of England from James II's wife onwards were very partial to a cup of tea.

So eating and drinking like a king, even an extravagant medieval monarch, is simpler and often cheaper than you might have imagined.

MICHÈLE BROWN

THE : NORMANS

WILLIAM THE CONQUEROR

(1066–1087)

✢ ✢

WHEN THE NORMANS, under Duke William, conquered Britain they brought with them a new order – not just in politics and administration, but in the related spheres of eating, drinking and entertainment. William was canny enough to realize that a well-fed and watered group of nobles and courtiers, constantly distracted by the festivities provided by a sumptuous court, was not so likely to cause him any trouble. Before setting out for the Battle of Hastings, William held a magnificent feast, and once he was established over here he inaugurated three major feast days in the year to which anyone who was anyone was invited. At Christmas a feast was always held at Gloucester, the Easter feast was at Winchester and at Whitsun the court celebrated at

11

Westminster. Clearly William recognized a good public relations exercise when he saw it, for he is generally supposed to have had himself crowned three times in order to hold three coronation feasts. On these occasions he was able to unwind and show himself as a genial host rather than a harsh dictator.

Although one chronicler of the time, probably seeking to ingratiate himself into the royal scene, described him as sparing in his eating and drinking and despising drunkenness, the consensus of opinion is rather different. William was greedy. Although physically strong and brave, his drawbacks included baldness, money-grasping and 'a protuberance of belly', which deformed his royal person somewhat. He liked his food well cooked and the story goes that when his favourite courtier, William Fitz-Osborne, who was steward of his household, served him with a roast crane which was very underdone, William had to be physically restrained from killing him. Clearly then, this was a man who took his food very seriously.

In the Domesday Book, compiled in William's reign, Robert Argyllon, the King's cook, is recorded as having been given a considerable tract of land, at Addington in Surrey, as a reward for presenting William with a dish called *dillegrout*, at his coronation. It was a sort of spiced gruel, rather like frumenty. The custom became established that whoever held that particular land afterwards had to present *dillegrout* to the new monarch at the coronation in order to be confirmed in his tenure. This ritual was still carried out nearly eight hundred years later at the coronation of George IV.

Although the Normans re-introduced into Britain a standard of cooking that hadn't been enjoyed since the Romans left some eight hundred years previously, their cuisine was limited by the lack of spices available. Vegetables were not greatly thought of; the major part of William's diet was made up of fresh meat. Game was abundant in the great untouched forests which still covered Britain, and which the King shrewdly made his own personal property. Chicken was a luxury, as it remained until present-day methods of production were introduced, and so was rice, which was not generally available until over one hundred years later. Recipes were also limited to some extent in that they had to result in something which could be eaten with the fingers, and with the aid of a knife, but no fork. Small wonder that the final instruction on most recipes of the time is 'and so messe it forth'!

✣

BLANK MANNG OF CHYKEN

Blancmange, which we nowadays take to mean a sweetened and fruit-flavoured custard, was originally a savoury dish. Savoury, that is, in the medieval sense, for rather as in present-day oriental cooking, medieval recipes frequently combined sweet and savoury tastes. The medieval equivalent of our blancmange would have been fruit-flavoured junket. The word blancmange seemed to settle down into its present meaning in the middle of the eighteenth century, and the initial confusion may have arisen because medieval people ate both sweet and savoury rice puddings.

1 boiling chicken, about	*lard or oil for frying*
1.35 kg (3 lb)	*salt*
1 onion, skinned	*fresh parsley*
1 bouquet garni	
seasoning	*FOR THE ALMOND MILK:*
225 g (8 oz) short grain rice	*1 litre (2 pints) water*
50 g (2 oz) butter	*225 g (8 oz) ground or*
12 g (½ oz) castor sugar	*pounded almonds*
50 g (2 oz) ground almonds	*1 teaspoon castor sugar*
50 g (2 oz) blanched almonds	

Make the almond milk by simmering the almonds gently in the water and sugar until all the flavour is extracted (this takes about 1½ hours). Strain.

Place the chicken in a large saucepan, cover with boiling water, add the onion, bouquet garni and seasoning. Cover, bring to the boil and simmer until the bird is tender. (About 1½-2 hours, according to age and size.) When cooked, remove from the stock, discard the skin and bones, cut the flesh into bite-sized pieces and keep warm.

Cook the rice in the almond milk, adding some of the chicken stock to make up the required amount of liquid. Drain the rice but do not dry it – it should be moist. Return the rice to the saucepan and add the diced chicken, butter, sugar and ground almonds. Season well.

Fry the whole almonds lightly in the oil or fat until golden. Sprinkle with a little salt. Serve the rice on a heated dish, decorated with the fried almonds and parsley.

SERVES 4

A typical dish from the first course of a meal at this time was brawn, which is best served with mustard. William's cooks would have created it into elaborate shapes – the most typical was a castle, complete with battlements and keep. Something sweet would have been served with each of the courses. It is likely that William would have enjoyed whole pears or quinces, sweetened with honey, and baked whole in individual 'cofynnes', as pastry cases were then called.

✦

WILLIAM RUFUS

(1087–1100)

✣ ✣

WILLIAM II, known as William Rufus because of his red-gold hair, inherited many of his father's characteristics. Like him he was personally courageous, he loved to entertain, he loved his food and as a result he was, like his father, 'somewhat big bellied'. Since both of them were rather squat, their waistlines cannot have contributed much to the dignity of their appearance.

But while William the Conqueror had managed to keep his vices under control his son was inclined to overdo it, becoming increasingly unpleasant as he got older. He was outrageously extravagant, and made himself unpopular by squeezing money unmercifully out of the rich and the poor alike. He spent this money wildly, disappointing people who had continued to hope he might suddenly display the more sterling qualities of his father. His court did not inspire respect. It was renowned for its women wrestlers, its ruffians and its general immorality; and considered to be a 'brothel of unlawful things, such as ought to be abolished'.

William's passion for spending money and his sense of his own importance were so great that he refused to eat, drink or wear anything unless it was *the* most expensive available. This seems to have been because he was completely without confidence in his own judgement, and had to rely on the price to tell him whether anything was worth having. It meant he was robbed left, right and centre by his servants, who exploited this foible to their own advantage. One morning, apparently, as he was drawing on a new pair of boots he asked his chamberlain what they had cost. On learning from the man that they had cost a mere three shillings he considered himself and his regal dignity deeply insulted, swore at the man and ordered him to bring a more expensive pair. The wily servant returned with an inferior pair of boots, telling him they had cost much more. The King was delighted, feeling that his honour had been satisfied, and the servant too was delighted, and quietly pocketed the difference.

William Rufus was mysteriously killed by an arrow while indulging in a favourite occupation, deer hunting, in one of the royal hunting parks, the New Forest. The mysterious circumstances surrounding his death have given rise to rumours of witchcraft and other dubious goings-on. It seems more likely however that someone who had been hounded for money for too long saw the opportunity of a way out and took it.

✣

VENISON WITH FRUMENTY

Venison was a popular dish with all medieval kings and William was no exception. He guarded his deer jealously, proclaiming that anyone who slew a hart should be blinded. A traditional accompaniment to boiled venison was frumenty, a rich and filling cereal dish. Frumenty can be sweetened with extra honey and enriched with more dried fruit and eggs to make a rich pudding something like a hot, medieval muesli. Frumenty in various forms is still made today, particularly in the West Country, although the name seems to have become altered to furmenty.

*1.35–1.8 kg (3–4lb) venison(ask
the butcher for a cut suitable
for boiling)
1 large turnip, sliced*

*3 carrots, sliced
3 onions, sliced
2 teaspoons parsley, chopped*

Place the meat in a large saucepan and cover with hot stock made from the bones of the deer or with hot salted water, using 1 level teaspoon salt to 500 ml (2 pints) water. Bring quickly to the boil to seal the meat, skim, and add the vegetables. Lower the heat and simmer until tender. (About 2–3 hours, depending on the size of the joint.)

Drain, leave in a warm oven for 5–10 minutes to dry off, then slice the meat. Serve with frumenty and a little of the strained cooking liquid.

If you prefer roasted venison cook 1.35–1.8 kg (3–4 lb) haunch or saddle of venison in a medium oven 180°C (350°F)/Gas 4 for 20 minutes per 450 g (1 lb), basting frequently with melted butter.

*FOR THE FRUMENTY:
100 g (4 oz) kibbled, pearled or
hulled wheat (from health
food shops)
325 ml (13 fl oz) approx. rich
full cream milk*

*25 g (1 oz) mixed dried fruit
1 beaten egg yolk
1 teaspoon honey
2 teaspoon ground cinnamon
salt*

Soak the wheat for 12 hours, or overnight, in water, preferably placing the bowl in a warm place. Drain. Boil the wheat gently in the milk for 20 minutes, add the dried fruit and continue boiling gently for another 40 minutes. Beat the egg yolk with the honey and cinnamon and stir into the wheat and milk.

Add a little extra milk if the mixture appears too stiff, but don't let it get runny. The grains of wheat should be soft. Season very sparingly with salt. If you make the frumenty in advance add extra milk when reheated.

SERVES 4

ḢENRY I

(1100–1135)

✢ ✢

ṈNLIKE HIS FATHER and grandfather Henry I was literate, or so
he liked to imply, and this was considered so unusual and
commendable that he was given the additional name of Beauclerc
by his people. He was of middling height, with black hair. This
hair was rather thin, a family trait, and Henry was brawny, tending
to fat – another family trait. One rather unctuous chronicler says of
him that he was plain in his diet, eating only when he was hungry,
and drinking only when he was thirsty. If this was so then he was
about the only member of his family to escape a third trait – greed.
The same chronicler neatly gets around the rumours of Henry's
lust, which was well known and much spoken of, by saying that
this was simply for the sake of issue (his only legitimate son,
William, was drowned in the wreck of the White Ship on his way
back from Normandy) and therefore he could not be accounted
the passive slave of lust but a definite master of his natural incli-
nations! If this was really Henry's intention he was most

successful and his wife, the pious Matilda, most patient, for he acknowledged some twenty illegitimate offspring and there were probably others.

It is easy to understand why Henry's subjects felt the need for circumspection when talking of him for he was ruthless and cruel in pursuit of his aims. As a young man he had personally thrown a Norman rebel from the battlements of a high castle to his death on the stones below. He had money lenders mutilated whether or not they were guilty of any misdemeanour, and he was prone to plucking out the eyes of his relations, including two granddaughters held as hostages, after their father had done something similar to William's hostages. His elder brother, Robert, from whom Henry had taken the throne, probably considered himself lucky merely to be held captive for twenty-eight years.

Henry's favourite food was lamprey, although it always disagreed with him. A lamprey is a long scaleless type of fish, not unlike eel, which attaches itself to stones on the river bed by means of suckers. It is now comparatively rare. Until about the middle of the seventeenth century lampreys were accounted a great delicacy and were popular with most monarchs. Kitchen inventories list special small silver pans for frying them. Lampreys used to be found in the Thames, but the best were considered to come from the River Severn, and the best method of cooking them was supposed to be the way they were cooked locally in Gloucester. The court always spent Christmas at Gloucester, and although lampreys were really out of season then, and not at their best, the loyal citizens of the city would always present the monarch with an elaborate lamprey pie. When the custom of spending Christmas at Gloucester died out, the city continued to send a lamprey pie to the monarch, wherever he or she happened to be at Christmas. This custom continued almost unbroken until the early part of Queen Victoria's reign.

Henry eventually died from a surfeit of his beloved lampreys, having disregarded his physicians' advice to steer clear of them.

Fortunately for the reputation of Gloucester the death was due to French lampreys eaten while Henry was fighting in France.

✣

LAMPREY IN BREWET

A pie cooked for the 1953 coronation by the Royal Air Force Catering Corps was based on the traditional method and contained cooked lamprey and hard-boiled eggs bound together with an aspic jelly delicately flavoured with claret. The amount of pastry for the crust required 4.5 kg (10 lb) of flour! However, lampreys were not used only in pies, and what pies there were were not often on the scale of the Christmas offering. In fact lampreys can be cooked quite simply, and most recipes for eels are suitable for lampreys, bearing in mind that lampreys need only half the cooking time of eels. Equally, recipes for lampreys can be made with eels and eel can be substituted for lamprey in the following recipe.

1 good sized lamprey (or eel)
about 5 cm (2 in) in diameter
150 g (5 oz) butter
½ teaspoon ground ginger
½ teaspoon cloves

salt and pepper
75 ml (3 fl oz) white wine
1 tablespoon mixed sweet herbs,
chopped

Leave the lamprey to soak for about 4 hours in salted water. Drain and wash well. Parcook in boiling salted water for 15 minutes (eel will take another 10 minutes or so). Drain, allow to cool. Skin and cut into chunks about 3.5 cm (1½ in) thick.

Melt the butter in a heavy pan with the spices and seasoning and fry the lamprey for about 5 minutes on either side (eel will need a little longer). Add the wine and herbs to the pan and bring to the boil, scraping up all the pan juices. Adjust the seasoning.

Serve the lamprey with the pan juices accompanied by hot white bread. This makes a delicious supper dish, and can be followed by *Quyncys in Comfyte* (see p. 71).

SERVES 2–3

STEPHEN

(1135–1154)

❖ ❖

THE REIGN of Stephen has not captured the imagination of the public or of historians. The nephew of Henry I, his entire reign was coloured by the battles he had to fight with Henry's daughter, Matilda, in order to keep his crown. Stephen of course felt he had right on his side, for it was generally assumed and agreed that no woman had the right to rule England, and certainly couldn't manage it if she tried. Matilda was eventually forced to withdraw her claim, though her son, the future Henry II, was made the official heir to the throne. The irony is that she would probably have made a far better job of ruling than her cousin, whose reign, so the chronicles say, was 'nothing but strife, evil and robbery'.

Stephen's problem was that he was far too good-natured and easy-going. He allowed his mighty subjects to walk all over him, taking advantage of his weakness to commit terrible crimes mainly motivated by greed.

What influence Stephen *did* have would not have been personal but derived from deference to his position as king. He would have needed to use all the tricks employed by his predecessors to make himself look impressive. Meal times were an ideal opportunity to bolster the reputation of a king, for they provided an occasion for pomp and ceremony. The Normans usually ate two meals in the day and both of them were leisurely affairs. There were three courses, five for very grand feasts. A course could comprise as many as a dozen different dishes, mainly savouries, roast meats and pies, with a few sweet dishes included, and what you ate was probably decided by what happened to be put in your immediate vicinity on the long table. Food was served on trenchers, very thick slices of bread. It is probably as a result of this custom that the English still eat so many things on toast. In the course of a meal up to half a dozen trenchers might be needed as they became rather soggy. At the end of the meal the remains, including these bread trenchers, were used to feed the servants, anything remaining after that going to the poor who thronged around the royal household waiting for alms. Bread was served separately, in addition to the trencher. It was because these scraps were later passed on that it has always been considered polite to break the bread into small pieces before eating it, rather than contaminating the whole lot, which you might not finish. Because of this and because there was one trencher between two people, manners were greatly emphasized. It was quite rightly considered anti-social to blow your nose with the fingers you might then be dipping into the communal food, or to fondle your dog's ears between mouthfuls. But medieval courtesy went beyond the immediately practical, for etiquette also forbade telling stories that might embarrass or shame another guest.

The king would sit at a separate table or at the very head of the table. Of course he would not be expected to share a trencher. At his place there would be a nef, a beautifully made container of costly metal, usually taking the form of a ship. This would contain a personal knife, spoon and goblet, a napkin, elaborately folded, a toothpick, and salt and spices. Both salt and spices were highly prized. The salt in particular was so valuable that your social rank was made apparent by whether or not you were seated above or below the elaborate salt cellar provided for the rest of those eating the meal.

The importance of the king was underlined by the ceremonial of his meal. He was served by his nobles, each with a specific responsibility: his Carver, his Cup Bearer and so on. Each of these would be accompanied by a troop of mortals of ever diminishing status, arriving eventually at a real servant who actually did something constructive. Anyone approaching the king would then be expected to retreat without turning his back on him. Perhaps most important of all was the Taster, for medieval kings had an obsession about being poisoned. The king's nef would usually contain a piece of narwhal which was considered to have magic properties for detecting poison. All this elaborate ceremonial together with lavish hospitality would help to imbue even an insignificant personality like Stephen's with a certain amount of royal splendour. With a strong monarch the ceremonial could become almost religious.

Pygge in Barre

For a king like Stephen, not only *how* he ate but *what* he ate would be an important prop to his position. The following recipe can also be used for roasting a whole, weaned pig, which would be even more impressive. The pig was brought to the king's table slung on bars of gold and silver. A frequent ingredient in medieval recipes was verjous, the unfermented juice of crab apples. Slightly sweetened cider vinegar makes an acceptable substitute.

FOR THE STUFFING:
50 g (2 oz) lard
50 g (2 oz) fresh breadcrumbs
2 beaten eggs
salt and white pepper
6 tablespoons mixed chopped
    fresh herbs (parsley, mint,
    sage, thyme)
¼ teaspoon saffron powder

1 sucking pig, about 3.65–4.5 kg
    (8–10 lb)
salt and white pepper
melted fat for basting
12 g (½ oz) fresh, white
    breadcrumbs
verjous (cider vinegar with a
    little sugar)

Mix the stuffing ingredients, season well. Season the inside of the pig well and stuff with the mixture. Sew up or skewer the opening. Rub the skin with salt and place in a preheated oven, 200°C (400°F)/Gas 6 for 30 minutes. Reduce the heat and continue cooking until the meat is thoroughly cooked. (About 4 hours or more.) Turn the pig over twice during this time. If the centre appears cooked before the ends, wrap foil around the middle of the pig and continue cooking. If the skin does not seem sufficiently crisp remove the foil and cook in a very hot oven 230°C (450°F)/Gas 8 for the last 10 minutes.

When the pig is cooked transfer it to a hot serving dish and keep warm. Pour excess fat off the meat juices, and stir the breadcrumbs into the remainder to thicken it. Season well, sharpen to taste with the cider vinegar and serve with the pig.

SERVES 8

✤

THE ⋮ PLANTAGENETS ⋮

ḣENRY II

(1154–1189)

✣ ✣

THE FIRST COOKERY BOOK written in Britain dates from the reign of Henry II. It was the work of Alexander of Neckham, and like most cookery books up to and including Mrs Beeton's, there is great emphasis on things medicinal. Henry, however, was not interested in food, and ate sparingly to combat his inherited tendency to run to fat. In fact he tended to despise any form of physical well-being as a sign of effeteness and was so restless and anxious to be active, particularly if it involved fighting, that he could scarcely bring himself to sit through a meal. His overriding preoccupation was going to war, and he even invented mock wars to keep his soldiers on active manoeuvres, rushing his troops off to Brittany and Normandy whenever possible. His unfortunate court was never allowed to settle anywhere, but was constantly on the move from residence to residence, complete with all the essential paraphernalia which was needed to keep the King in the appropriate, impressive style. The strain of keeping things running smoothly must have been tremendous, for Henry, like all the rest of his family, had a foul temper and when angered he would throw himself to the ground in paroxysms of rage and chew the rushes or his mattress. It was Henry's hot temper which led to the murder of Thomas à Becket.

Apart from war, Henry's main interests were music, literature and women. His reputation as a womaniser was well known among his subjects, and he is even rumoured to have had an affair with his prospective daughter-in-law. He met his match in the woman he married, Eleanor of Aquitaine, who was tough and strong-willed as well as beautiful. She had previously been married to King Louis VII of France and it was said that while accompanying him on a crusade she had indulged in what was, according to the chronicler, 'the worst kind of licentiousness – carnal familiarity with a Turk'.

A long-lasting legend arose about the way in which she dealt with her husband's favourite mistress, 'fair Rosamund', whom he kept in a labyrinthlike house at Woodstock for her own protection. The King, when he left his mistress's chamber on one occasion, trailed a silken thread after him, which had caught on his foot. Eleanor followed the thread, found fair Rosamund and dealt with her summarily, for she was never seen alive again. Henry had his revenge many years later, when, disguising himself as a friar to hear her deathbed confession, he was able to elicit all the details of Eleanor's affairs and deal equally ruthlessly with the men.

With all the other activities at court, it is not surprising to learn that the standard of food at Henry's court was atrocious. Nobody cared enough about it. A letter written from the court by Peter of Blois describes the wine as being so full of dregs that noblemen were compelled to close their eyes and filter it through their teeth. Fish was sold in a stinking condition and the tables were piled high with putrid food. Peter of Blois concludes that it was only because the courtiers kept themselves so healthy with vigorous exercise in the fresh air that many more of them did not die of food poisoning. Medieval cookery books reveal quite unashamedly the lack of concern for what we would consider basic hygiene. There was no pretence that the dishes arrived at table untouched by human hand. One recipe for soup advises that while it cooks one man be assigned to keep an eye on it and blow on the gravy. Another gives a method for preventing the age-old problem of a sinking pie crust. First make a little hole in the pie crust, '& at that hoole, blow in the cofynne (pie) with thin mowth a gode blaste of Wynde; and sodenly stoppe the hole, that the wynd abyde withynne to reyse uppe the cofynne, that he falle nowt a-dowune'.

✧

VYNE GRACE
A SPICY PORK CASSEROLE

3–4 tablespoons olive oil	350 g (¾ lb) onions, sliced
675 g (1½ lb) pork fillet, cubed	salt and pepper
flour	2 tablespoons malt vinegar
½ teaspoon ground ginger	250 ml (½ pint) white wine
¼ teaspoon white pepper	125 ml (¼ pint) light stock

Heat the olive oil, coat the pork cubes in seasoned flour and fry quickly on all sides to seal. Remove meat from the pan, lower the heat and cook the ginger and the white pepper in the oil for about 2 minutes, stirring continuously.

Place the meat and onion in alternating layers in a casserole, seasoning each layer well. Stir the vinegar, wine and stock into the spices in the frying pan, scraping up all the pan juices. Pour this sauce over the meat and onion in the casserole. Cover and cook in a warm oven 160°C (325°F)/Gas 3 until tender (2½ hours approx). Before serving check seasoning and sharpen with a little extra malt vinegar to taste. Serve with plain boiled rice and a side salad.

SERVES 4

RICHARD I

(1189–1199)

✣ ✣

RICHARD I was a handsome man, addicted to soldiering and
revelling in the camaraderie of the field. He was idolized by
his subjects and nicknamed 'Coeur de Lion', the Lion-Hearted.
He had little time for any women, including his wife Berengaria,
who never once set foot in England; but he was devoted to his
mother, Eleanor of Aquitaine. She had a powerful personality and
dominated her son. When, after an initial period of domestic bliss,
Eleanor and her husband Henry had clashed irrevocably, she took
up the cudgels on behalf of her favourite son and caused endless
trouble between him and his father. When Richard eventually
came to the throne he spent only six months of his ten-year reign
in England. So it seems curious that it was during his reign that
people saw something of a revolution in English cookery that was
indirectly due to the King himself.

28

Richard was full of crusading zeal, for *real* crusades, and he spent the major part of his time harrying the hapless infidel in the Middle East. The history books abound with tales of his deeds against the evil Saracen Saladin. His rescue after two years of captivity by his faithful friend and minstrel Blondel, who sang beneath the walls of endless impregnable castles until he heard his master's answering refrain, has become something of a legend. During Richard's absence the future 'Bad King John', sworn foe of the legendary Robin Hood, was plotting his downfall. When news of Richard's release was brought to England one of John's fellow conspirators was so terrified he dropped dead with fright.

Contact with the enemy and their civilization led to the introduction of many new customs and habits – for instance Arabic numerals took the place of the clumsier Roman system. Travellers also brought back new tastes in food and the ingredients to achieve them. There had always been some spices available for the kitchens of the wealthy but there was now a greater variety than ever. As well as ginger, cinnamon and nutmeg there were cloves, galingal, cubebs, coriander, cumin, cardamom and aniseed, to name but a few. Apricots, damsons, dates, figs, lemons and pomegranates became more familiar. The result was a highly spiced type of cookery not unlike Indian food today. The similarity becomes more marked when you consider that, just as people in hot climates today make great use of spices to compensate for the fact that food deteriorates quickly, so our medieval ancestors, without the benefits of refrigerators, would have been grateful for the strong spicy flavours to mask more dubious flavours. Because recipes of the time seem to use a prodigious amount of spice it might be assumed that the newly opened spice routes had reduced the prices and made them a commonplace. This was definitely far from the case. Spices remained luxury items, highly prized and stored away under lock and key. Cookery books were written for wealthy households; the rest of the population would have eaten very plain food indeed. Even salt was so highly prized that a supply was kept guarded in a specially constructed building in the Tower of London.

Apart from their value for flavouring food, spices were considered invaluable for curing and preventing diseases, so that the spice box was also the equivalent of the medicine chest. Ginger was thought to strengthen the teeth and prevent toothache; nutmeg was good for the brain and the eyes; pepper could cope with almost anything from dysentery (the scourge of the crusaders) to bubonic plague. Coriander was used as an aphrodisiac. It may or may not be true that cannibalism was practised by the Christian soldiers during their campaigns, but it is certainly true that English cooking, like that of other Western European countries, underwent a considerable change at this time.

✢

LECHE LUMBARDE

Today we eat Indian curry followed by small, incredibly sticky sweets. The highly spiced dishes of the Middle Ages were also followed by very sweet sweets, perhaps more reminiscent of Greek desserts than Indian ones. They are unusual, delicious and very rich. *Leche Lumbarde is* a comparatively simple recipe and I have given the original as well as the modernized version to give an idea of what the cookery books of the Middle Ages contained. Many medieval recipes contain the word 'leche', which means slice. At least one recipe book has a section devoted to *Leche Metys* – sweet and savoury dishes which were served cut into slices.

Take Datys an do a-way the stonys, & sethe in swete Wyne; take hem uppe, an grynd hem in a mortere; draw uppe thorw a straynoure with a lytyl whyte Wyne & Sugre, And caste hem on a potte, & let boyle tylle it be styff; then take yt uppe, & ley it on a borde; than take pouder of Gyngere & Canelle, & wryng it, & molde it to-gederys in thin hondys, & make it so styf that it wolle be lechyd; & if it be not styf y-nowe, take hard yolkys of Eyron & kreme ther-on, or ellys grated brede, & make it thike ynow; then take clareye, & caste ther-on in manner of a Syryppe, when thou shalt serve it forth.

225 g (8 oz) stoned dates	*175 g (6 oz) breadcrumbs*
18 g (¾ oz) castor sugar	
250 ml (10 fl oz) sweet white wine	*FOR THE SYRUP:*
¾ teaspoon ground ginger	*250 ml (10 fl oz) claret*
1 teaspoon ground cinnamon	*6 tablespoons honey*

Mince the dates and place them in a heavy saucepan with the sugar and enough wine to cover them. Simmer gently for a few minutes until the dates soften and the sugar dissolves. Press through a sieve. Return to the pan and cook very gently until most of the liquid has evaporated (about 15 minutes). Allow to cool.

Mix in the spices and enough of the breadcrumbs to form a stiff paste. Press into a greased tray, so that the mixture is about 3.5 cm (1½ in) deep. Leave in a cool place overnight to firm up.

Serve in thin slices with a syrup made by reducing the claret with the honey and leaving it to cool.

SERVES 8

✣

After the period of the Crusades there were several recipes with the word 'Sareson' in the name. Begin the meal with *Brewet Sareson*. This is a thick creamy soup made by boiling rice flour in almond milk (see p. 12) with plenty of minced cooked chicken and pork. Season it well and flavour to taste with ground ginger and sugar. As a meat course serve *Crustardes of Flessh* (meat pie). This is made by parboiling pigeons in verjous (unfermented crab apple juice; sweetened cider vinegar makes a reasonable substitute). The flesh is then taken off the bones, mixed with raisins, currants, salt, spices and beaten eggs and baked under a pie crust.

✣

KING JOHN

(1199–1216)

✢ ✢

KING JOHN, Richard's brother, the unfavourite child of his
mother, earned himself the additional title of 'Bad King
John'. He was the wicked, grasping foe of Robin Hood, the evil
monarch defeated by the 'good side' and made to sign the Magna
Carta. Few historians found anything good to say about him,
which makes one suspect that he can't have been all bad! On the
plus side must be counted the fact that, unlike the majority of his
contemporaries, he enjoyed frequent baths. No wonder they
decided that there *must* be something wrong with him.

Like his illustrious forebears he enjoyed a reputation for glut-
tony and lechery. Henry I had died of a surfeit of lampreys: King
John died of a surfeit of peaches and new ale. This can only have
confirmed current thinking that eating fruit was bad for you. Right
until the seventeenth century eating fruit was considered a haz-
ardous undertaking. Sir Thomas Elyot, in a book called *The Castel
of Health* dated 1539, wrote that 'Fruites generally are noyfulls

(annoying) to man, and do engender ylle humours' – though one may reasonably doubt this opinion since he also declared that peaches 'do make better juyce in the bodys for they are not too soone corrupted beyng eaten'. If fruit was eaten at all it was to be at the beginning of a meal, followed by a good spicy stew to counteract the 'frigidity' of the fruit. No one would have been surprised that John met such a nasty end for not only did he eat his peaches as a between-meal snack, but they were raw as well!

Modern thinking would be more inclined to see his death as an indication of the poor quality of the fruit of the time. Although many varieties existed, they would have been small and puny – wild fruit really. It was not until the sixteenth century that gardeners like Henry VIII's began cultivating fruit to improve its size and quality rather than merely growing the original variety. It was probably the resulting improvement which gradually decreased the suspicion in which all fruits were undoubtedly held.

As well as his greed John seems to have inherited a foul temper. Like Henry II before him he would chew the floor coverings in his rage, and in addition he would come out in vivid blue spots. He was avaricious and gloated over his jewels, so it can hardly have improved his temper when the whole lot was lost in the Wellstream estuary. It is in keeping with his character that he ignored the elaborate and numerous religious fast days which required either total fasting or a fish diet. It is also in keeping with his character that he exacted everything due to him. Undeterred by the fate of Henry I, he fined the men of Gloucester forty marks because 'they did not pay him sufficient respect in the matter of his lampreys'. Perhaps strangest of all the dues he extracted was two hundred chickens from the wife of Hugh de Neville, his chief forester, in order that 'she may lie with her husband for one night'.

We get an idea of the scale of cooking going on in the King's household from the accounts, which relate, for example, that fifteen thousand herring, one thousand eels, a thousand pounds of almonds and five thousand eggs were ordered for various

Christmas feasts. The vast number of eggs (old recipes beginning 'Take two dozen eggs' have become something of a culinary joke), was not just a reflection of the large numbers catered for. Eggs, like fruit, would have been very small compared with those we are used to.

CHIK FARSED AND ENDORED, WITH SAWCE NOYRE

Endoring, or gilding, a dish with a mixture of egg yolks and spices was a frequent practice in medieval cookery. The more brightly coloured the food the more it was prized, and the chicken should be a bright unabashed yellow. Medieval cooking had standard sauces for certain dishes, just as we tend to expect mint sauce with lamb or horseradish sauce with beef. The standard sauce for roast chicken was *Sawce Noyre* (Black Sauce) so called because it was made with liver. The standard sauce for boiled chicken was *Sause Blaunk* (White Sauce) made with ground almonds. The names come from the Norman French, which was considered to have more 'ton' than the English, rather as we have French menus in English restaurants now. The spelling was variable.

*1 roasting chicken, about 1.35 kg
  (3 lb)
100 g (4 oz) butter for basting*

*FOR THE STUFFING:
1 small bunch parsley
6 hard-boiled egg yolks
25 g (1 oz) shredded suet*

*1 level teaspoon sage
12 g (½ oz) currants
½ teaspoon ground ginger
½ teaspoon ground cinnamon
½ teaspoon ground cardamom
¼ teaspoon saffron powder
salt and white pepper*

Blanch the parsley in boiling water, drain and chop it small. Mash the egg yolks, combine with the remaining ingredients, and season with salt and pepper to taste.

FOR THE SAUCE:
50 g (2 oz) chicken livers
5 tablespoons white breadcrumbs
½ teaspoon ground ginger
½ teaspoon ground cinnamon
small pinch aniseed

½ teaspoon salt
small pinch white pepper
½ teaspoon sugar
200–250 ml (8–10 fl oz) water
cider vinegar

Cook the chicken livers in the oven with the chicken for about 10 minutes, until cooked but soft inside. Mince them up with the breadcrumbs. Place in a saucepan with the spices, seasoning, sugar, cooking juices from the chicken, and half the water. Bring to the boil, stirring, gradually adding the rest of the water until the required consistency is reached. If the sauce is reheated more water will be needed. Check seasoning, and sharpen with a little cider vinegar to taste. Prepare the sauce at the last possible minute, as it should be served immediately.

FOR THE GLAZE:
2 egg yolks
½ teaspoon sieved flour

¼ teaspoon saffron powder
½ teaspoon ground ginger
salt and white pepper

Beat the ingredients together into a thickish batter.

Stuff the chicken. Rub the skin with butter and roast it in a fairly hot oven 190°C (375°F)/Gas 5 until cooked. (About 1–1½ hours.) Remove from the oven. Pour off the cooking juices to complete the sauce. Paint the chicken all over with the glaze, using a pastry brush. Return the chicken to the oven and leave the glaze to set in a warm oven 160°C (325°F)/Gas 3 without browning.

Garnish the chicken with fresh parsley, and serve the sauce separately.

SERVES 2–3

✤

HENRY III

(1216–1272)

✤ ✤

HENRY CAME to the throne when he was only nine, and grew to be a gentle young man, passionately fond of architecture and the arts, and a great patron of the Church. He rebuilt Westminster Abbey almost entirely and left it looking much as it does today. He revelled not only in magnificent buildings but also in beautiful clothes and jewels and in the ceremonial and feasting that were an integral part of court life. However, his charity did not just extend to giving money for rich church buildings. He had a genuine compassion for the poor and needy and gave away huge sums of money as alms. One of his many good deeds was the institution of an annual feast for the poor in the Great Hall of Windsor Castle itself. All in all Henry seems to have been surprisingly free of the vices of his forefathers, and even acquired a reputation as a good husband and father.

Unfortunately he would have been more impressive to his peers, the barons, if he had been more of a tough, soldierlike figure obsessed by war and greed. Nor did his physical appearance make up for what he lacked as a dominant personality, for he was rather short and had one drooping eyelid. He irritated the barons by showing a distinct preference for foreigners as his advisers, despite the fact that in every other respect he was intensely English and extremely proud of his Anglo-Saxon ancestry. As a result the barons rebelled and Henry became involved in a long-drawn-out fight with them, and with Simon de Montfort in particular.

Life went on at court much as usual despite the fighting, and in a normal day the King's household consumed an enormous quantity of food. Like his namesake Henry II, the King was inordinately fond of lampreys. The large number consumed was partly a result of the many meatless days which had to be observed. Henry, unlike his father, would not have dreamed of breaking the rules. Indeed he was rather abstemious and forbade more than two dishes of meat at ordinary meals. So the royal cooks were faced with the usual problem of making a fast seem like a feast, with a variety of fish which included porpoise, whale, pike, sturgeon, mullet, tench, turbot, oysters, crab, lobster, sole, plaice and trout to name but a few. To ensure his supply of lampreys the King had his own weirs on the River Severn and forbade any trade in lampreys during periods of short supply 'until John, his cook, has taken all he needs for the King's use'. Queen Eleanor sent in separate orders for her own household. We know that the cooks of Gloucester had not lost their magic with the local delicacy for in 1242 we read that the Bailiffs of Gloucester were 'commanded to send pasties of salmon and lampreys as quickly and frequently as they can to the king'!

✧

PASTIES OF SALMON

Until our rivers became so polluted salmon was a comparatively common fish. The recipe uses verjous (see also page 23) which was an essential component of many recipes, and which was used right into the seventeenth century.

750 ml (1½ pints) almond milk (see p. 12) made with 1 litre (2 pints) water to 225 g (8 oz) almonds
675 g (1½ lb) fresh salmon, thinly sliced
25 ml (1 fl oz) verjous (cider vinegar with a little sugar)

450 g (1 lb) (flour weight) puff pastry
½ tablespoon castor sugar
salt and white pepper
50 g (2 oz) blanched almonds
12 g (½ oz) butter
1 beaten egg yolk

If the almond milk has greatly reduced make it up to 750 ml (1½ pints) with a little water. Poach the salmon slices in the almond milk and verjous until tender. (About 20 minutes.) Allow to cool. Drain and reserve about 125 ml (¼ pint) of the cooking liquid.

Roll out the pastry and cut two squares approximately 20 x 20 cm (8 x 8 in). Flake the salmon and place half in the centre of each pastry square. Sprinkle with sugar, salt and white pepper. Moisten with a little of the cooking liquid.

Fry the almonds gently in the butter until golden. Drain. Put a layer of almonds on the fish. Gather the corners of the pastry to the centre to form two square envelopes. Moisten the edges with a pastry brush dipped in the cooking liquid and press them together securely. Decorate the pasties with leaf shapes cut from any remaining pastry. Brush with beaten egg yolk, and cook in a moderate oven 190°C (375°F)/ Gas 5, until the pastry is golden (about 35 minutes). Serve hot or cold.

SERVES 8

✤

These pasties are delicious served with watercress salad (see p. 53). Begin the meal with *Soupes Dorroy*, an onion soup made with a wine and beef stock and served with croûtons. A typical pudding would be rice, cooked in almond milk and honey and served with a sweetened compote of apples or pears.

ᴇDWARD I

(1272–1307)

❖ ❖

ᴇDWARD I's nicknames included 'Longshanks', because of his great height, and later 'Hammer of the Scots'. Most of his life he was busy hammering someone; if it was not the Scots, it was the Welsh. He wanted to subdue all opposition. It was he who initiated the custom of creating the eldest son of the monarch Prince of Wales, when he gave his son Edward that title. In Scotland he was embroiled in a long-drawn-out fight which never really came to anything, especially when he eventually found himself up against Robert the Bruce. This was the Scottish king who was inspired by the tenacity of a spider spinning its web, to resolve never to give in, least of all to the English. However Edward did strike a blow for English morale by walking off with the Stone of Scone, the traditional seat on which the Scottish kings were crowned, and symbolically placing it beneath the English coronation seat in Westminster Abbey. All in all Edward was a man to fear. As a youth it was said he had put out an eye and cut off the ear of a man who had had the temerity simply to cross his path. The family bad temper and insistence on getting their rights was definitely prominent in his nature.

Although a great warrior and formidable opponent, there was a softer side to Edward's nature. He was devoted to his wife, Eleanor of Castile. When she died he was heartbroken. At every town where her body had rested overnight on its journey from Lincoln to Westminster he raised a cross, the last being at Charing Cross, London.

During Edward's reign Brie was imported from France for the first time, and haddock was listed in the household accounts. Perhaps Edward brought back a taste for this fish from his Scottish campaigns. He may also have come across whisky, or *uisge beatha* (water of life) as it was then known in the original Gaelic. Sturgeon became the royal fish, and was exclusively reserved for the royal table, Edward insisting on his rights again. Edward may have been more civilized than his fighting ways would lead us to believe, for a fork was itemized in his household inventory. Forks were almost unheard of at that time, and they did not become everyday household items for four hundred years or so. Queen Anne, who died at the beginning of the eighteenth century, usually ate with her fingers. Edward's fork was probably some sort of cooking utensil like a toasting fork. The state of English teeth then as now was abysmal, and the chances are that anything solid enough to be raised to the mouth on a fork would probably be too tough to chew when it got there. The tendency continued to be for mushy foods which could be eaten with a spoon or neatly packed into the pastry cases called 'cofynnes' or 'trapes'.

TARTE DE BRY

This cheese tart should be eaten immediately, while it is still hot, as it puffs up rather dramatically. Like a soufflé, it is delicious cold as well, but not quite so impressive to look at. It could be made with any of the soft cheeses of Northern France. A cheese tart like this would be eaten on one of the seemingly unending fast days that medieval religious practice required. Nowadays it makes a delicious savoury ending to a meal – an interesting change from the usual pudding and a novel way of eating the cheese. The pastry could be either shortcrust or puff pastry – medieval cookery books give recipes for both. For a lighter crust, use 175 g (6 oz) pastry and roll it out thinly.

225 g (8 oz) (flour weight) rich
  shortcrust or puff pastry
225 g (8 oz) very ripe Brie
  cheese, scraped from its crust
single cream

2 beaten eggs
1½ teaspoons castor sugar
1 level teaspoon ground ginger
¼ teaspoon saffron powder
salt

Line a 20 cm (8 in) flan dish with the pastry and bake 'blind' for 10–15 minutes at 220°C (425°F)/Gas 7. Allow to cool.

Melt the cheese slowly in the top of a double boiler, adding a little cream if it seems lumpy. Add the beaten eggs and the seasoning, mixing thoroughly. Pour the mixture into the pastry case and bake in a fairly hot oven 190°C (375°F)/Gas 5 for about 30 minutes until lightly browned and puffy. Serve immediately.

SERVES 4–6

✛

EDWARD II

(1307–1327)

✣ ✣

EDWARD II might at first sight have seemed ideal kingly material. He was young, good-looking, fond of sports like wrestling, swimming, racing and hunting, and fond of drinking with his friends. His father, however, suspected that his son was not the stuff that good kings were made of, and he turned out to be right. Edward II's natural friendliness and willingness to be led developed into something rather more extreme when he came first under the influence of Piers Gaveston, and then of Hugh le Despenser. His nobles took exception to his associations and so did his young Queen, Isabella, who was only twelve when she arrived from France to marry him. When the situation became too humiliating for Isabella she led a rebellion which ended in her husband's murder.

Fortunately Edward could not see into the future, and much of the time his court was full of jollity and entertainment, for if his friends were poor politicians they were witty and funloving companions. Nevertheless Gaveston, who was in charge of the coronation feast, made a poor job of it, for the food was not properly cooked, and what there was was cold.

At this time minstrels, jesters and story-tellers were an essential part of the court and its festivities, and were on familiar terms with the King – coming near to an equality and acceptance that many of his nobles would not be allowed to achieve. The Whitsun feast of 1316 was held, as was now the custom, in the magnificent Great Hall at Westminster, built by William Rufus. A woman who wanted to petition the King for some favour or other disguised herself as a minstrel and rode on a magnificently apparelled horse right up to the King's table, where she was able to lay her petition directly before him. The guards at the door had not even questioned her presence, for minstrels came and went as they pleased in all the courts of Europe.

✣

DARYOLS

The word 'daryol', and the dish itself, originated in France. Today it is more commonly spelt dariole, and dariole moulds are often used, particularly for the little cakes called madeleines, even though darioles themselves are not often made. However, this type of egg custard tart has survived in a more prosaic form, and versions of it were noted in recipe books for many hundreds of years after the medieval version first appeared. Although related to plain egg custard it usually contains a permutation of more exotic ingredients such as wine, fresh strawberries, dates, almonds, cloves, mace and bone marrow – each recipe varies slightly. Although it is unlikely that the originals were the same shape, dariole moulds are rightly named after these pastries, for the pastry cases need to be deeper than usual so that the fruits are covered by a deep layer of the custard mixture. One recipe says 'Do it in a cofynne of two ynche depe; bake it wel, and serve it forth.' Of course the deeper the pastry case the richer the whole thing would be.

Consistent with the medieval tradition, the appearance was as important as the taste, and individual tartlets were often made in a variety of colours by adding red and green vegetable colouring to two-thirds of the custard mixture and using saffron only in the remaining third, which would be bright yellow. If you prefer a lighter crust, use 175 g (6 oz) pastry.

*225 g (8 oz) (flour weight) rich
    shortcrust or puff pastry*
*75 ml (3 fl oz) sweet white wine
    such as Barsac*
500 ml (1 pint) double cream
4 egg yolks, beaten
1 blade mace

¼ teaspoon ground ginger
2 cloves
1 sachet saffron strands
100 g (4 oz) dates, finely chopped
*100 g (4 oz) fresh or frozen
    strawberries*
2 teaspoons castor sugar (optional)

Line one 20cm (8in) flan dish or six individual flan dishes (ramekin dishes would be ideal) with the pastry. Bake 'blind' for about 15 minutes at 220°C (425°F)/Gas 7. Allow to cool.

Put the wine, cream, egg yolks and spices in the top of a double boiler and cook gently, stirring until the mixture begins to thicken. Allow to cool. Place chopped dates and whole strawberries in the flan case, allowing one strawberry for each individual tart. Cover the fruit with the strained custard mixture. Bake in a moderate oven 180°C (350°F)/Gas 4 until the custard is set. (About 25 minutes.) Serve hot or cold.

SERVES 6

✧

As a main course for this period serve roast goose, stuffed with whole cloves of garlic. This could be accompanied by *Spynoches Yfryed*. Squeeze the moisture out of spinach which has been softened by boiling for a couple of minutes, and then fry it in oil and season it well. Begin with *Brewet of Lombardye*, a chicken soup coloured bright red with vegetable colouring and thickened with fresh breadcrumbs and beaten eggs.

✧

EDWARD III

(1327–1377)

✢ ✢

EDWARD III proved a welcome relief after his father for he was
endowed with all the virtues any Englishman could expect
of his king. He was brave, wise, merciful, chivalrous, courteous, a
successful military leader and a patron of learning. His reign
seemed to incorporate the best of all worlds with Chaucer writing
his poetry and the Black Prince performing amazing deeds of
courage and daring. English prestige was high because of successful wars in France. One of the most famous of these battles was
the English victory at Crècy. There is a type of carrot soup, called
Crècy or Cressy soup, apparently named after this battle, which
was fought over the farmlands of Northern France where carrots,
among other things, were growing.

Edward was a king who revelled in the trappings of monarchy:
the feasting, the jousting (at which he excelled) and the reverence
paid to women, who were greatly romanticized as 'Damoiselles of
Exquisite Beauty and Purity'. At the tournaments a knight would

wear a favour – a ribbon or similar token given by the lady of his choice – to bring him luck in the contest and to flatter her that his deeds of derring-do were only possible because of her inspiration. Edward deliberately encouraged this almost fairy-tale atmosphere at his court, partly because it suited his nature, partly because an essential element of the whole image was unswerving loyalty to the king. The coronation feast of his Queen, Philippa of Hainault, was followed by festivities lasting three weeks with jousting, dancing, singing and feasting every day.

After one particularly successful tournament at Windsor Castle, at which all the mighty of the land were gathered for an Arthurian occasion of jousting, feasting and romantic dalliance, Edward came up with the notion of a revival of the Knights of the Round Table. As a venture it never really came to anything, but the ideals of Romance and Chivalry undoubtedly permeated the whole of Edward's thinking about his role as king.

The Round Table may not have survived as a viable idea, but Edward was responsible for another body of knights which was to become equally renowned – the Knights of the Order of the Garter. It was an élite of the twenty-five greatest men in the land. A garter was one of the favours frequently worn by knights while jousting, so the name is not quite as bizarre as it seems to us today. There are several versions of how it all came about. The most well-known story is that the King was dancing with Joane, Countess of Salisbury, when her garter slipped down her leg and Edward, chivalrous as always, made the famous remark *Honi soit qui mal y pense*, which became the motto of the Order. An alternative story says that the Queen's garter fell off while she was dancing and that the famous line was her response to some remarks of Edward's. There is probably no truth in either story. Surprisingly the garter is not worn by women members of the Order; they sport a sash across the left shoulder instead.

His fondness of show did not mean that Edward was unaware of the virtues of economy; or at least economy that other people could practise. He issued a statute forbidding anyone, whatever his rank, to have more than two courses at dinner or more than two dishes in each course, three being allowed for special festivals. Since some grand occasions traditionally warranted as many as eighteen dishes in each course this was quite a severe edict. Edward's reasons were that 'the great men by these excesses have been sore grieved', presumably by indigestion or over-spending, while the poor were impoverishing themselves still further by trying to imitate their betters. We do not know if the new rules were ever really obeyed.

Doubtless the rich, suffering from over-indulgence, would have been grateful for the large-scale cultivation of saffron which developed in this country during Edward's reign, particularly in the area of Saffron Walden. According to the medical lore of the day saffron was an aid to the digestion, kept you fit and happy and was also beneficial in restoring strength to weak limbs and regulating the liver.

At this time also, the cause of cooking was being advanced by the first of the great French chefs, Guillaume Tirel, better known as Taillevent. He had begun as a kitchen boy and ended his days as Master Chef to the kings of France. He became a wealthy man, for good cooks were prized and rewarded on both sides of the Channel. He was elevated from his lowly rank and given a family coat-of-arms which rather quaintly incorporated six roses and three cooking pots. He collected his recipes into a manuscript cookery book entitled *Le Viandier* (The Gourmet), which tallies very closely with contemporary English cookery books. This similarity between English and French food was to continue for several hundred years.

✜

BEEF Y STYWD WITH MACROWS

This recipe is for a hot and spicy stew almost reminiscent of a curry. Breadcrumbs are used to thicken it, and breadcrumbs or blood were the main thickening agents used until the eighteenth century, although a liaison of egg yolks and cream might be used in sweet dishes. Macrows is the medieval equivalent of macaroni, and was served with a dish such as beef stew and also on its own with cheese and butter just as we eat it today.

1.35 kg (3 lb) ribs of beef or 900 g
 (2 lb) stewing beef plus bones
 for stock
1.5 litres (3 pints) water
1 bouquet garni
1 onion, sliced
1 carrot, sliced
salt and pepper
2 onions, finely chopped
2 tablespoons fresh parsley,
 chopped
1 teaspoon dried sage

½ teaspoon white pepper
2 teaspoons ground cinnamon
1 teaspoon pepper corns, ½
 teaspoon cloves and 3 blades
 mace, tied in a small muslin
 bag
35–50 ml (1½–2 fl oz) malt
 vinegar
1 small brown loaf, crusts
 removed
½ teaspoon saffron powder
chopped parsley to serve

If using ribs of beef first bone them. Boil the bones in the water with the bouquet garni, sliced onion, sliced carrot and seasoning, until reduced to about 1 litre (2 pints). (About 2½ hours.) Strain.

Cube the meat. Simmer the meat in the stock with the onions, herbs and seasoning, and all the spices except the saffron, until the meat is tender. (About 2¾ hours.) Skim from time to time. When the meat has been cooking for about 1 hour take 250 ml (½ pint) of the stock and add it to the malt vinegar. Soak the bread in this liquid.

When the meat is cooked, remove the bag of spices and add the soaked bread and the saffron powder to the stew. Bring to the boil, stirring, and simmer until the liquid thickens and the saffron colour develops. Adjust the seasoning.

Sprinkle thickly with fresh parsley and serve with macaroni.
SERVES 6–8
✤

RICHARD II

(1377–1399)

✢ ✢

RICHARD II was another English king who had the misfortune to come to the throne while still a child. He had the additional disadvantage that his father, the Black Prince, had had such a wonderful reputation that he could only seem inadequate in comparison. He was handsome, and he could on occasions be courageous, but on the whole he struck his courtiers as effeminate and often extremely cruel. Having been King for most of his life he had a grossly exaggerated opinion of his own worth. He did not think much of the sort of people who enjoyed the supposedly manly arts of jousting, fighting and hunting. In return they did not think much of the sort of man who was so refined in his habits that he invented the handkerchief, rather than make do with his fingers or his sleeve.

It is unlikely that Richard would have allowed anything to soil his clothes which he loved dearly and which were always richly encrusted with gold and gems. It was a time when the most elab-

orate and exaggerated dress was in fashion. The ladies shaved
their heads to give the impression of a high forehead, which was
considered particularly beautiful. This was then emphasized by
tall, horned and cone-shaped headdresses from which hung flim-
sy veils. While the women strove after a pure, uncluttered profile
their men were wearing elaborately curled and powdered hair.
Both sexes loaded their hands with rings. Stylish men wore
incredibly long-pointed shoes, which in many cases were so
impractical they had to be supported by delicate chains attached
to the wearer's legs. It was a social phenomenon not unlike the
long fingernails of the Chinese Mandarins or Elizabethan ruffs. By
sporting such a totally impractical fashion the wearer proclaims
himself as someone who did not need to be equipped for the prosaic, servile tasks of life. He set himself apart from ordinary
people. Richard's first wife, Anne of Bohemia, is said to have
invented the side-saddle, another impractical fashion, made necessary by impractical clothes.

Richard's court was famous not only for its extreme fashion but
for its entertainment. Things had changed rather from the days
when the courts were entertained by roaming minstrels, singing
long unaccompanied epic ballads telling of past chivalrous deeds.
The new-style court entertainment was rowdy, irreverent and not
a little vulgar. Richard's favourite jester was a particularly bawdy
individual called Scoggin, whose jokes and stories were more
coarse than funny. Elaborate pageants and tableaux heavy with
symbolism were also popular. Much of the meaning of these
entertainments would be lost on us today, but those watching
were steeped in the allegorical implications of everything they
saw. One occasion for this type of production was the marriage of
Richard to his second wife, Isabel, daughter of the King of France.
Richard had been desolated by the death of Anne of Bohemia and
his marriage to Isabel, a seven-year-old child, was simply a diplomatic manoeuvre which necessitated as much ostentatious display
as possible. On her ceremonial entry into Paris the little princess

was faced with a large scale model of a castle, in which was a richly covered bed, the 'Bed of Justice', containing a figure supposed to be St Anne. Singing birds and other small animals were part of the tableau, together with a white hart, a lion, an eagle and twelve maidens with swords in their hands, ready to defend the 'Bed of Justice'.

Hospitality was on a phenomenal scale at any court, but even so, Richard's court was considered exceptional. The Christmas festivities of 1399 were held in William Rufus's Great Hall in Westminster, which Richard had just finished rebuilding. So many people were catered for (one estimate put it at ten thousand daily) that twenty-eight oxen, three hundred sheep and untold quantities of poultry were consumed every day. During feasting of this kind, valuable presents were presented to the King and to his guests. A constant supply of wine was another mark of lavish hospitality. At Richard's coronation a pillar, crowned by a gilt eagle, turned out to be hollow and became a fountain continuously dispensing wine to rich and poor alike.

Richard is supposed to have employed some two thousand cooks. It was some of this number who compiled the first true English cookery book *The Forme of Cury* (cookery), containing one hundred and ninety-six recipes and an index for easy reference. It was dedicated to Richard 'the best and ryallest vyand of all Christian kings'. 'Vyand' means a nice eater or gourmet and is the English equivalent of the word used in the title of Taillevent's French cookery book *Le Viandier*. *The Forme of Cury* is notable for the variety of its recipes, which include a salad, and their similarity to the French recipes. Much of the terminology is French as well. Once the initial barrier of the language is overcome it is remarkable how similar many of the recipes are to the ones we use today. However, quantities and cooking times are rarely specified so a cook using them would have been experienced and skilled enough to guess these for himself. A saying of the time goes, 'God may send a man good meate but the devyll send an evyll cooke.'

A skilled chef was therefore a respected and wealthy man. Naturally the warmest seat in the kitchen was reserved for him and he would probably work largely in a supervisory capacity. Contemporary illustrations show the cook carrying a large wooden spoon for tasting various dishes and for clouting the ears of lazy kitchen boys. Richard obviously treated his cooks with the correct respect and deference, and they equally respected his good taste in food. Ironically it is suspected that Henry IV, who deposed Richard, allowed him to be starved to death in Pontefract Castle.

✣

PEJONS YSTEWED

2 tablespoons fresh parsley, chopped

1 teaspoon fresh thyme, chopped

salt

10 cloves garlic, peeled

2 pigeons, drawn and trussed

50 g (2 oz) lard

750 ml (1½ pints) freshly made game or chicken stock

1 teaspoon ground ginger

1 teaspoon white pepper

½ teaspoon powdered saffron

25 g (1 oz) white breadcrumbs

1½ tablespoons verjous (cider vinegar with a little sugar)

2 thick slices buttered toast to serve

Season the herbs with salt, and stuff the pigeons with the herbs and whole cloves of garlic. Melt the lard and fry the pigeons quickly on all sides.

Place the pigeons in a large saucepan, cover with stock, spices (except the saffron) and seasoning. Poach gently until tender. (About 50 minutes.) Remove the pigeons and keep them warm.

Add the saffron to the cooking liquid and reduce it to about half the quantity by boiling rapidly. Add the breadcrumbs, and cook for a further 2 minutes. Sharpen with verjous to taste. Adjust seasoning.

Serve each pigeon on a slice of toast with the sauce poured over it. This dish needs no vegetable accompaniment.

SERVES 2

SALAT

1 piece fennel, root and leaves	1 teaspoon fresh rue, chopped
1 small leek	salt
2 shallots	½ tablespoon fresh mint, chopped
2 cloves garlic	½ tablespoon fresh sage, chopped
1 tablespoon fresh parsley, chopped	1 teaspoon fresh rosemary leaves
	4 tablespoons olive oil
1 tablespoon borage leaves, chopped	2 large bunches watercress
	malt vinegar to taste

Chop the fennel, leek, shallots and garlic and combine in an earthenware bowl with the fresh herbs. Sprinkle with salt and add the olive oil. Leave for about an hour, turning the vegetables in the oil from time to time. Wash and dry the watercress.

Just before serving tear up the watercress and add it to the oil and herb mixture. Do this at the last possible moment so that it remains crisp. Sprinkle with a little malt vinegar to taste. Adjust the seasoning as necessary and serve.

This watercress salad makes an unusual appetiser to the meal, and is very good served on a bed of undressed lettuce leaves. It is also a good accompaniment for fish and any dish, such as *Pome Dorreng*, which does not have a sauce of its own. As a sweet course serve *Peris in Comfyte* (see p. 63).

✣

ḣENRY IV

(1399–1413)

✛ ✛

ḣENRY'S LIFE as King of England was not a very happy experience, partly because he was consumed with guilt for usurping his cousin Richard. In his will he calls himself a 'sinful wretch'. He became an old man prematurely, and was a prey to morbid fancies. Yet as a young man he had been a fearless soldier and as fond of merriment as anyone.

Although already beginning to feel the trials of kingship weighing upon him, Henry gave a magnificent feast on the occasion of his coronation. It was really an impressive public relations exercise to convince the world that he was a strong and wealthy king. Today a medieval feast is often called a banquet, but the word was not in use for about another eighty years when the Middle Ages were almost past. When it was first used it did not mean a sumptuous meal, but a separate course of sweets, fruit and wine, eaten in a room apart to which only a few guests were invited. It long continued to be a custom for guests who were not intimate friends of the family to withdraw politely at this dessert stage in the meal. Banquet as a term for a sumptuous feast began to come into use during the next century presumably because of the association of rich sweet things with a special treat or occasion.

We know exactly what was served at Henry's coronation feast because the menu was noted down. There were nearly forty different dishes, divided into three courses, each containing both sweet and savoury dishes. At the end of each course is listed a *sotelte* (subtlety), an ornate table decoration made from sweet almond paste rather like marzipan. This would either be placed in the centre of the table as the different dishes of each course were brought in, or brought in by itself at the end of the course in order to be duly admired. A *sotelte* could be almost any shape or subject. Popular themes were ships in full sail, which gave ample scope for the cook's artistry; scenes from the lives of the saints; and scenes symbolic of the monarch's life and virtues. They were beautifully painted in the bright, primary colours so popular at the time, or better still they glittered with real gold leaf. As skills increased they were even given mechanisms, and one French king proudly presented a *sotelte* in which a model of his wife went through the motions of giving birth to their heir. Needless to say these *soteltes* were not intended to be eaten.

Among the dishes that *were* meant to be eaten, one or two seem unusual to modern eyes. Eagle, cygnet, heron, crane and peacock no longer feature on our tables. The popularity of these birds was due to their appearance more than their taste. Even medieval opinion of peacock meat was pretty low. 'Peacock is evyll flesh to disiest (digest), for it cannot be roasted or soden ynough.' However the peacock, served in its exotic plumage, was usually the highlight of the meal. It was customary for it to be carried to the high table by the most beautiful lady at the feast, accompanied by a group of musicians. To add to the theatrical effect, a piece of cloth dipped in spirit would be placed in its beak and set alight. The way to prepare a peacock was as follows.

At a feeste roiall pecokkes shall be dight in this Manere. Take and flee off the skynne with the fedurs, tayle and nekke, and the hed thereon; then take the skyn with all the fedurs, and lay hit on a table abrode; and straw thereon grounden comyn; then take the pecokke, and roste hym and endore hym with rawe yolkes of eggs; and when he is rosted, take hym of, and let hym coole awhile, and take and sowe hym in his skyn, and gilde his combe, and so serve hym forthe with the last cours.

In private homes eating was becoming less of a public spectacle than it had been when everyone ate together in the great hall of the castle and the servants and dogs vied with one another for the scraps. Public functions, however, continued to be very public indeed, and the coronation feast which lasted many hours was watched by an audience not invited actually to partake of the meal itself. Henry himself was passionately fond of good music and his own musicians entertained at the feast but it is hard to see how a fairground atmosphere could have been avoided as the occasion wore on, and it seems unlikely that many of the guests would have observed one of the basic rules of medieval etiquette which held that you should wait until the meal was over before getting intoxicated! After the meal came the dancing, much disapproved of by the staider elements of society, who considered the new dances from Italy and France quite scandalous. This stage in the events was probably greatly enjoyed by Henry's son, the Prince of Wales, who had spent the first part of the festivities serving his father.

✣

POME DORRENG

Pome dorreng means golden apple and it has been one of the traditional recipes of England since the Middle Ages. It would have been a welcome relief at the coronation feast where the food consisted largely of roasted meats. The 'apples' should be bright yellow outside and pale inside, so egg white and not whole egg is used for binding the meat. Sometimes half of them would be rolled

in fresh parsley and a combination of green and yellow 'apples'
sent to the table. Either way it is essential not to overcook them in
the last stage or the colours will simply become a uniform brown.

550 g (1¼ lb) minced pork fillet	*FOR THE GLAZE:*
1 heaped teaspoon castor sugar	*4 egg yolks*
½ teaspoon salt	*50 ml (2 fl oz) almond milk (see*
½ teaspoon white pepper	*page 12) made with 50 g (2 oz)*
1 egg white	*almonds to 250 ml (10 fl oz)*
1 litre (2 pints) chicken stock	*water*
melted fat for cooking	*1 level teaspoon castor sugar*
fresh parsley to serve	*75 g (3 oz) flour*
	small pinch salt

Mix together the pork, sugar and seasoning. Bind with the egg
white. Divide the mixture into sixteen and form into 'apples'.
Heat the stock and place the 'apples' of pork gently into it using
a spoon. Simmer them very gently for 10 minutes, remove from
the stock and leave to cool.

Thread the meat onto skewers, four 'apples' for each person.
Brush the meat with plenty of melted fat, and grill at a very high
temperature, turning frequently so they are evenly cooked, and
brushing the meat frequently with melted fat to keep it moist.
When the meat is cooked through, brush the 'apples' with a thick
coating of the blended glaze, lower the temperature of the grill,
and continue cooking just long enough for the glaze to set – do not
allow it to discolour. Serve immediately on a bed of well-buttered
boiled rice. Garnish with plenty of fresh parsley.

SERVES 4

✣

Watercress salad (see page 53) goes well with *Pome Dorreng*. To follow serve *Quyncys in Comfyte* (see page 63), one of the few sweet
dishes served at Henry's coronation feast. Begin the meal with
plain boiled shrimps, sprinkled with vinegar and served with
wholemeal bread and butter.

ḥENRY V

(1413–1422)

✤ ✤

ḥENRY V made himself one of the great heroes of English history by bringing the French to their knees and then dying young before the tables turned and he could be blamed. His funeral was one of the grandest ever staged, with three of his warhorses being led up to the altar of Westminster Abbey to take part.

Shakespeare has depicted him as a likeable rapscallion and rogue who led a wild, fun-loving youth and then pulled himself together on the death of his father to become 'a Good King'. A good king he may have been, but the attractive scapegrace sowing his wild oats seems to be pure imagination. Henry seems to have been rather dull and lacking in humour, interested only in man's business, war. His skill at waging war made him greatly admired by his fellow countrymen but he can't have been much fun to live with. Shakespeare created a wonderful scene in which he woos his future wife Katherine with a great deal of charm. In reality he married her because she was the defeated French King's daughter and he saw her as a way of getting the French throne as well as the English one. After one day's honeymoon he was off to *really* enjoy himself on a good campaign. He did take time off to bring her back to be crowned in England but was back in France again within a few months. Not long after his death Katherine secretly married the Clerk of the Wardrobe, a Welshman called Owen Tudor with whom she may have been consoling herself before. It was their family which produced the famous Tudor monarchs including Henry VIII and Elizabeth I.

Given Henry V's character and reputation as a bit of a goody-goody, we are not surprised to learn from the chroniclers that there was:

> No man more moderate in eating and drinking, with diet not delicate but rather more meat for men of war than for princes or tender stomachs. Every honest person was permitted to come to him, sitting at a meal, where either secretly or openly to declare his mind.

We have records of several of his meals, including the feast following the coronation of Queen Katherine. This took place in February 1421 which was Lent and so the menu was almost entirely of fish dishes. The *soteltes* at each course were heavy with symbolism. at the very end of the meal there was a *sotelte* of the Queen's namesake, Saint Katherine, holding a motto proclaiming an end to war through this sacred marriage. It did not really reflect what Henry had in mind.

✤

ᵱYKE IN ᴇRBAGE

This dish was part of the first course at Katherine's coronation feast. Pike was greatly prized by the kings of the Middle Ages. It has a very delicate flavour and it is difficult to understand why it is now so neglected, except perhaps because it has rather a lot of fine bones which have to be negotiated while eating. *Pyke in Erbage* (pike with herbs) has oysters in the stuffing. Oysters were abundant at this time and eaten by rich and poor, even as late as the nineteenth century. English oysters were considered to be particularly good.

The roe of the pike should not be eaten.

1 pike about 1.35 kg (3 lb)
125 ml (5 fl oz) claret
1 anchovy, finely chopped
100 g (4 oz) butter

FOR THE STUFFING:
6 oysters
25 g (1 oz) butter for frying

salt and pepper
½ teaspoon ground nutmeg
1 large onion, minced
1 clove garlic, crushed
2 sprigs rosemary
2 teaspoons fresh thyme, chopped
2 teaspoons fresh marjoram,
   chopped

Wash the pike thoroughly, but do not remove the scales.

Shell the oysters and fry them lightly in butter. Season with salt, pepper and ground nutmeg. Stuff the pike with the oysters, onion, garlic and herbs. Secure the opening by tying or skewering.

Season the fish and place it in a baking tray with the claret, butter and anchovy. Bake uncovered in a hot oven 200°C (400°F)/Gas 6, basting very frequently, until cooked. (About 40 minutes.)

Serve immediately with a little of the stuffing and cooking juices spooned onto each portion.

SERVES 4

The pike is best served with plain boiled rice and a green salad. Begin with fried whiting, also served at the coronation feast, and complete the meal with *Daryols* (see page 43).

✢

ꜧENRY VI

(1422–1461)

✣ ✣

ENRY VI was a gentle, unworldly, almost simple man totally unfitted to be king in the ruthless age in which he lived. He had a reputation for holiness and good works, and attempts were even made after his death to have him canonized as a saint. To his courtiers' amazement he always made them remove their swords before entering church, and at a time when it was common practice to chat throughout the service, Henry insisted on silence. He was a great patron of learning and founded many schools and colleges, notably King's College, Cambridge, and Eton School. The boys from Eton would pay visits to nearby Windsor Castle where the King often stopped to speak to them, usually giving them gifts of money with the words, 'Be good lads, meek and docile, and attend to your religion.' His heart just was not in a job which seemed to require so much cruelty. On one occasion he was disgusted and appalled to see the bits of a man hanged and quartered for treason stuck up on a spike, so he immediately pardoned everyone else accused of the same crime. Other more successful monarchs would not have been so soft-hearted. Nor would his wife, the redoubtable Margaret of Anjou, who encouraged her seven-year-old son to pronounce the death sentence on a group of men who had held her husband prisoner. But Margaret's toughness could not compensate for Henry's weakness and he was eventually overthrown by the Earl of March who became Edward IV.

In some ways Henry's unworldliness made him rather quaint, particularly on the subject of nudity, which he found 'a great offence'. The idea of getting totally undressed to take a bath struck him as shocking. He enjoyed the company of women, whom he found more sympathetic than men, but he was horrified by any immodesty of dress, including the fashionable décolletage of the time. If a lady in a low cut dress came anywhere near him he would run away in embarrassment and horror crying 'Fie! Fie! for shame'. One of his crueller courtiers once brought to court a 'floor show' of ladies in very low cut dresses indeed, just to see the King's reaction.

During Henry's reign there appeared two books which are interesting for the light they shed on the domestic life of the time. One is the *Boke of Curtasye* (1430), which has a long list of the do's and don't's of medieval etiquette, including advice to take special care of where you spit in the presence of a man of God. The second is the *Liber Cure Cocorum*, containing one hundred and twenty-seven recipes all written in rather bad verse. It is not a royal cookery book but includes many rather more down-to-earth recipes, if verse recipes can ever be considered down to earth. From other documents it seems clear that, as with the Normans some four hundred years before, two meals was the norm for a royal or aristocratic household, both of them long-drawn-out affairs. A light meal might be eaten on rising, but the first real meal of the day was at about eleven o'clock in the morning, the equivalent of our lunch time. At five o'clock there would be supper, and of course most people would retire to bed fairly early except during the light summer evenings. After the meal had been eaten and cleared away a complete second sitting would follow for the staff and lesser dependents of the court or household.

QUYNCYS OR PERIS IN COMFYTE

Henry VI was only eight years old when he was crowned in Westminster Abbey on 6 November 1492, but like any monarch he was not spared the hours of feasting and ritual which followed. As part of the first course. which also included *Frument with Venison* and the inevitable peacock in its feathers, *Quyncys in Comfyte* were served. This was obviously considered a great delicacy as it is one of the few sweet things listed in other similar feasts. It is a spicy fruit salad, which should be served very cold. Some recipes also suggest pears as an alternative. Wardouns (wardens), a very old variety of cooking pear, are often specified in recipes and the word came to be almost synonymous with the word pear.

65 g (2½ oz) whole stem ginger	*225 g (8 oz) stoned dates*
75 ml (3 fl oz) sherry	*1 level teaspoon ground ginger*
4 quinces or large, firm pears	*2 level teaspoons ground*
225 g (8 oz) castor sugar	*cinnamon*
550 ml (22 fl oz) red wine	*small pinch salt*

Cut the stem ginger into thin slices and leave to soak in the sherry in a covered jar for three days.

Peel the quinces or pears and slice them across to form rounds about 0.5 cm (¼ in) thick. Remove the core from each slice of the fruit. Dissolve the sugar gently in the wine and cook without boiling until the mixture starts to thicken. (About 15 minutes.) Add the sliced fruit to the wine and simmer gently until cooked, but still firm. (About 10 minutes.) Add the dates, spices and salt, and continue heating without boiling until the flavours are thoroughly blended. Add more sugar if necessary. The mixture should be a fairly syrupy consistency. Leave to cool. Strain the ginger slices, reserving a tablespoon of the liquid. Stir this liquid and the ginger into the wine syrup. Chill and serve.

SERVES 6

✤

EDWARD IV

(1461–1483)

✥ ✥

EDWARD IV was handsome and charming. In an age when tall people were something of a rarity he towered above his contemporaries, measuring as he did six feet four inches. His grandson Henry VIII inherited his great height. Edward exploited his good looks and attractive personality to the utmost, to bring back to the court and monarch a more impressive and powerful image. All the household arrangements and entertaining were organized with this in mind and aimed at giving the courtiers such a good time that they would not want to disturb the *status quo*. Keeping up appearances was not always easy when there were noblemen in the country with just about as much money to spend as the King. When a group of Bohemian ambassadors visited London in 1466 Edward pulled out all the stops to entertain them, regaling them with a feast of some fifty different dishes. The following day they were entertained by a nobleman who offered them a choice of sixty.

In the main Edward succeeded in getting over the right image. This was particularly true once his new wife, Elizabeth Woodville, brought her influence to bear on court ritual. She had a rather flashy sense of style and managed to bring to the English court something of a continental flavour. Elaborate hunting expeditions were organized at which splendid picnics were served in silken tents. Midnight jousts were held by torchlight, followed by feasting and dancing. Edward excelled at dancing and cut a dashing figure. Queen Elizabeth was deeply disliked by many people who regarded her as an interfering upstart. She was the sort of woman they might have expected to be Edward's mistress but not England's Queen. A rumour was current in court that in fact Edward *had* intended her to be simply his mistress but Elizabeth was so determined to be Queen of England that she refused to give in even when he held a knife to her throat. Edward was so besotted by her he was forced to compromise and marry her instead. Certainly she was a very strong-willed lady who was determined to receive the regal treatment that she felt was her due. Following her churching after the birth of her daughter a feast was held to which women only were invited, men being allowed in merely as spectators in the gallery. The occasion lasted three hours and Elizabeth kept her ladies-in-waiting kneeling the entire time.

Edward was keen to give a good impression of himself and his court but he was also keen to practise economy. His household accounts book, the *Black Book of the Household of Edward IV,* has survived and gives details of household expenditure and also of household duties. It even contains instructions to the people in charge of Edward's small son to 'see that he goes merry to his bed'. Expenses are calculated right down to the last candle. Edward was determined not to be sponged on and the *Black Book* also contains lists of those on the official roll, the 'bouche of court', which entitled them to be fed at the King's expense. Those who were not listed were liable to be humiliated publicly by being totally ignored by the servants as they sat at table. Edward was fond of music but the *Black Book* lists only thirteen minstrels on the official pay roll. Edward saved money by hiring freelances for occasions which warranted something slightly grander.

Printing was introduced into Europe at about this time and in Italy the first printed cookery book appeared, *De Honesta Voluptate,* by Platina. The recipes are said to be the work of a chef called Martino, for even then cookery was considered to be a job for male chefs rather than women. Clearly the regard which people had for cookery was quite considerable if cookery was the subject of one of the first printed books. The recipes now started to get more precise about quantities and method, but the book continues the tradition of incorporating a lot of medical advice including recommending a good hearty laugh as a cure for indigestion and other ailments. Medical advice and information were always popular as life was very uncertain and often short. Edward was so conscious of his health that while he ate a 'Doctoure of Physyque' sat by him to advise him on his diet.

ALOWS OF BEEF

In spite of the fame of the roast beef of old England, beef does not figure particularly noticeably in old recipe books. Maybe it was presumed that everyone would know how to roast it anyway. This dish is a little more complicated and is therefore noted in some detail. The same recipe may be used with mutton or lamb steaks cut from the leg. Beef marrow was a frequent ingredient of sweet and savoury dishes, used where we would tend to use suet or butter.

FOR THE STUFFING:
1 onion, minced
2 tablespoons fresh parsley, finely
   chopped
4 hard-boiled egg yolks
2 tablespoons shredded suet, or
   beef marrow
1 teaspoon ground ginger
pinch saffron powder
salt

4 minute steaks or very thin rump
   steaks

TO SERVE:
1 tablespoon verjous (cider vinegar
   with a little sugar)
2 teaspoon ground ginger
2 teaspoon ground cinnamon
freshly ground black pepper
2 hard-boiled egg yolks, crumbled

Combine the stuffing ingredients and season well. Spread a quarter of the mixture over the centre of each steak and roll it up like a pancake. Keep each steak in shape with a skewer. Brush the steaks with a little oil and cook under a hot, preheated grill for about 20 minutes, turning once. The steaks will be fairly rare in the centre if cooked for this length of time. Arrange the steaks on a heated serving dish. Pour a very little of the verjous on each. Sprinkle with the spices and crumbled egg yolks. Serve immediately.

SERVES 4

✤

Broccoli was introduced to England from Italy at about this time and it is very good served with the steaks. Begin the meal with fillets of John Dory dipped in batter and deep-fried. Serve *Leche Lumbarde* (see page 30) afterwards.

✤

RICHARD III

(1483–1485)

✦ ✦

RICHARD III, called 'Crouchback', has just about the worst reputation of any English king. He is reputed to have murdered Henry VI, his own brother the Duke of Clarence, and his brother Edward's two young sons – the young Edward V and his brother the Duke of York. However, another school of thought says he was a brave soldier, a wise administrator, a good friend to his brother Edward IV and far from being a deformed hunchback was an elegant courtier and a graceful dancer. Since the strong opinions originate with people who were not alive when Richard was King the truth can never be fully known and probably lies somewhere in between. He was eventually defeated by Henry Tudor at the Battle of Bosworth, where he fought with his precious crown on his head and where, according to Shakespeare at least, he uttered the immortal lines 'A horse, a horse. My kingdom for a horse.'

Richard was King for a very short time but in spite of the dubious circumstances surrounding his accession he was crowned with full pomp and splendour in Westminster Abbey, with the customary feast afterwards in Westminster Hall. This feast took place about four o'clock in the afternoon. The King sat at the high table with Queen Anne on his left and the Archbishop of Canterbury on his right. All the ladies sat at one table, the great Lords at another and there were further tables for lesser guests. The King ate off gold and silver dishes and the Queen off gilt dishes. These were served to them by high-ranking nobles like the Duke of Norfolk. The ceremony and ritual were elaborate and lengthy.

As the second course was brought in, the King's champion, Sir Robert Dymock, rode into the hall on a charger and offered to do battle on the King's behalf with anyone who had the temerity to question Richard's right to the throne. He then threw down his gauntlet according to the rules of chivalry and waited to see if anyone would take up the challenge. Of course no one did. Afterwards the champion was presented with wine in a jewelled goblet, and having taken a token drink from it he flung the remainder to the ground and departed with the goblet as a gift from the King. This did not occur just because Richard's claim to the throne was rather shaky. It was a custom that had been part of the coronation ritual for hundreds of years, and continued up to the nineteenth century. The challenger was always from the Dymock family and always uttered the same challenge. At the coronation of George IV in 1821 he came riding in on a white charger which he had borrowed from Astley's circus! A far cry from the days when the challenger would automatically be given the best horse in the King's stables.

The King's champion was not the only person to leave the feast with a valuable souvenir. The Lord Chamberlain came away with the basin and ewer which he had held for the King to wash his hands. The nobleman acting as chief butler would get the King's goblet, which was of gold with a gold lid. The ceremony was all so lengthy that though it began at four o'clock the chronicler tells us 'by that time that all was done it was dark night'.

BOR IN COUNFETT

This recipe distinctly specifies the flesh of the male pig, the boar. This flesh would probably have been rather tough and so needed to be softened with a marinade. Marinading the meat is unusual, and is not normally required in medieval recipes, even for venison which is usually marinaded before cooking. Richard's device as Duke of Gloucester was a wild boar, and wild pig, although gradually dying out, was still found in England, but domestic pigs were also kept for meat.

4 pieces of pork fillet, about 175 g (6 oz) each

1 onion, sliced
1 carrot, sliced

FOR THE MARINADE:
250 ml (½ pint) red wine
2 tablespoons olive oil
3 teaspoons honey
2 bay leaves
1 clove garlic, crushed

FOR THE SAUCE:
250 ml (½ pint) red wine
4 tablespoons honey
½ teaspoon white pepper
1 level teaspoon cloves
pinch of salt

Beat the pork fillet fairly flat. Combine the marinade ingredients and leave the meat to marinate for 3–4 hours, turning it from time to time and spooning the mixture over it.

Make the wine sauce by combining the ingredients in a saucepan and boiling gently until the flavours have had time to infuse and the liquid has reduced by about a third. Skim and strain.

Roast the pork in a covered dish for 35 minutes in a hot oven, 220°C (425°F)/Gas 7

Remove from the oven, drain off the fat, pour the sauce over the meat and continue cooking *uncovered* for a further 10–15 minutes at 180°C (350°F)/Gas 4. If the sauce starts to dry out add a little more red wine. Remove meat from the oven, allow to cool and serve very slightly chilled, with the sauce.

SERVES 4

ᒍENRY VII

(1485–1509)

✣ ✣

THERE IS a well-known portrait of Henry VII in which he looks like the original Kilroy, with little hands clutching on the edge of the frame as he peeps slyly from the picture. It sums up the character which he is said to have had – sly, tenacious and stingy. He looks as if there might be some truth in the allegation that it was he and not Richard III who murdered the little princes in the tower.

Sly and cunning he certainly was: it was one of the reasons for his success. He was also mean with his money, hoarding it and nurturing it so that when he died he left a fortune behind him, in marked contrast to most of his predecessors who tended to spend every penny. He did not choose to waste money on expensive wars, which, since people were impressed by military success, was a mistake if he wished to leave behind him not only money but a reputation as a great and resourceful monarch. But when he thought it would make a useful impression he would invest his money in an ostentatious display of wealth, deliberately encouraging expensive pageantry which would improve his status in the eyes of the world. The marriage of his son Prince Arthur was such an occasion and the event was celebrated with weeks of lavish hospitality, feasting, masques and pageants. The famous 'Beefeaters' were his idea, and a shrewd one too, for even today they are one of the most memorable elements of English court pageantry.

During his reign the first printed English cookery book was published, the *Noble Boke of Cookery ffor a Pryncis Household*. A few years later came *The Boke of Kervynge* (a handbook of carving) by the curiously named Wynkyn de Worde. Carving was an important task at any meal because the meat had to be suitable for eating with the fingers while still allowing the eater to maintain his dignity. An added difficulty was the almost total absence of forks at this time, so that the carver had to be able to hold the meat steady with his fingers as he carved it, and yet not overhandle it so that the guests were put off the food. De Worde says that no more than two fingers and a thumb may be used to keep the joint in position. *The Boke of Kervynge is* famous for the remarkable list of technical terms used by its author to describe the standard techniques for dressing and serving different meats and fish. A few examples are enough to get a feel of the brisk and rather ruthless terminology. 'Dysmember that heron, spoyle that henne, strynge that lampreye, barbe that lopster, disfygure that peacocke, wynge that quayle, tayme that crabbe, splat that pyke.'

The book also deals with the duties of several other household officials including the butler and the panter who were in charge of the cellars. After a meal it was a well-established custom to take a *voidee* of wine and spices, the equivalent really of a glass of port and chocolate mint today. The word originates from a French word meaning to empty, and the voidee was the last hospitality offered before the house was 'emptied' of its guests. Henry VII was always anxious to be a hospitable and *impressive* host and there are regulations in his household book to ensure that the butler and the keeper of the spicery had plenty of warning if anyone was going to stay for wine and spices. The regulations also laid down that these should be served from the very best dishes available. The mixture of wine and spices was known as hippocras or hypocras. There is a recipe for it in De Worde's book and also in the earlier cookery book *The Forme of Cury*. Basically the following spices were used: cinnamon, ginger, galingale, cloves, cardamom, pepper and aniseed. Sometimes sugar and dried fruit were added as well. The word hippocras comes from the Greek name Hippocrates. The spices were mixed into the wine according to individual taste, left in a warm place overnight, and then filtered out after the flavours had infused. An Hippocrates sleeve or bag was used as the filter, and this gave the drink its name.

When Henry's first wife died he sent his ambassadors round Europe looking for a suitable replacement. They came up with a possibility in the form of the Queen of Naples. His questions to these same ambassadors are often quoted, for among the instructions were 'to mark her breasts and paps, whether they be big or small', and 'to mark whether there appear any hair about her lips or not'. These enquiries occasionally give rise to the suggestion that Henry became something of a lecher in his old age. However, he would seem to have had his feet quite firmly on the ground for he also wished to know 'the manner of her diet, and whether she be a great feeder or drinker'. The reply came back 'The said Queen is a good feeder'. But despite this or maybe because of it the marriage did not eventually take place.

✜

LING – 'ẎELLOW AS A ĠOLD ŊOBLE'

Cod and ling were by this time a normal part of everyone's diet. Some of the fish came not from the seas around Britain, but from as far afield as the areas of North America discovered in the attempts to find the North-West Passage. There is some confusion as to what actually constitutes ling. There is a type of fish similar to cod known as ling. However, the name often seems to apply to

cod itself, the larger 'long' variety, especially if it has been salted
or dried, as much of the fish coming from more distant waters
must have been. Andrew Boorde, who wrote a book in 1562 called
A Compendyous Regymen or a Dyetary of Healthe says that ling is
accounted 'beefe of the sea', but even he is not sure exactly what
it is. He does say that the salted version is definitely called ling
and that when it is treated it becomes 'yellow as a gold noble', (a
golden coin). The same effect can be achieved by using the popular medieval spice saffron.

*4 ling or cod steaks, about 2.5 cm
(1 in) thick*
½ a peeled onion
salt and pepper
melted butter
100 g (4 oz) finely ground oatmeal
175 g (6 oz) butter for frying
1 parsnip, diced small
2½ onions, finely chopped
*2 tablespoons fresh herbs, chopped
(parsley, sage, marjoram etc.)*

FOR THE STOCK:
1 litre (2 pints) water
*450 g (1 lb) fish pieces and
trimmings*
1 onion, sliced
1 carrot, sliced
½ teaspoon saffron powder
1 bouquet garni
1 coffeespoon peppercorns
salt

Make the stock by boiling the ingredients gently for about 1 hour.
Strain. Rub the cut sides of the fish with the onion half. Season
the fish well. Brush with melted butter and coat thickly with oatmeal. Fry gently in butter until pale brown and slightly crisp on
both sides. Place fish in an ovenproof dish. Fry the parsnip and
onion in the remaining butter, then pack them round the fish, filling in the spaces with the chopped herbs. Season well. Fill the
dish carefully with the stock so that it just covers the fish. Cover
and bake at 180°C (350°F)/Gas 4 until the fish is tender. (About
40 minutes.) Do not overcook as the liquid will change from
yellow to brown.

SERVES 4

✣

ʰENRY VIII

(1509–1547)

❖ ❖

ENRY VIII was so handsome and talented that when he came
to the throne he was called the 'New Apollo'. He was a
wonderful dancer, a talented musician, able to play the recorder,
lute and virginals; he could hunt and joust better than anyone; he
was well-educated with a good mind and an infectious enthusiasm
for life. Six wives and a life of debauchery later he was a prematurely aged fifty year old, fat, gouty, bad-tempered and probably
suffering from syphilis. He was so heavy that he needed special
machinery, not simply to get him up on to his horse, but even to
get him upstairs. No longer lithe and athletic he had a fifty-four-
inch waist and his armour was constantly being let out to accommodate his ever-increasing girth. Behind the apparent grandeur of
his court there was squalor and dishonesty. The standard of
Henry's servants was at a very low ebb. They were dirty, thieving

and careless, inclined to steal the supplies and wipe their greasy fingers on the priceless tapestries hanging on the palace walls. Henry seems to have let the rigid household discipline of his father and grandfather become lax, and the court was crowded with greedy parasites, all entitled to food and 'perks' of one sort or another. One of the commonest rackets was to sell off the food, and it cannot have been difficult to make a tidy profit at the King's expense if, like the Lord Chamberlain, you were entitled to sixteen dishes at dinner.

But it was not all dirt and misdemeanour. During his reign and especially during his youth, Henry's court was the scene of many splendid feasts and entertainments. Everything, from the architecture to the food, benefited from continental influences as people began to travel more frequently. Italian ideas in particular were everywhere. There was certainly no evidence of economy. At the coronation of Anne Boleyn in June 1533 there were three courses, twenty-eight dishes in the first course, twenty-three dishes in the second and thirty in the third, 'besides subtleties and ships made of wax, marvellous gorgeous to behold'.

Henry loved an opportunity for dressing up and any entertainment which called for fancy dress. He gave 'bankets' to which guests had to come in the costumes of other nationalities. At one the ladies came dressed as Egyptians with their bodies covered in the sheerest black gauze 'so that the same bodies seemed to be nygrost or black Mores'. On another occasion the King and eleven of his nobles surprised the Queen and her ladies by appearing dressed like Robin Hood and his Merry Men, complete with hoods and bows and arrows.

The King enjoyed his food, too, and food was becoming more interesting, partly because there was a wider range. A far greater variety of foods was available than ever before, including turkeys from Mexico; and the New World was soon to provide other popular additions to the Englishman's diet. Peas were another innovation; carp was reintroduced into the country; marmalade was first noted, though it became more popular in Scotland than England; and the proper cultivation of fruits like apricots and apples was begun. A popular rhyme of the time goes,

> Turkies, carps, hoppes, piccarell and beere,
> Came into England all in one yeare.

It refers to one of the most fundamental changes in English diet, the introduction of hops and therefore the beginnings of beer as we know it today. Until then the words ale and beer had been synonymous for beer brewed without hops. From this time the old-style drink stayed as ale and the new style, which quickly became the more popular, was called beer.

A meal given by the King for thirty guests at Windsor Castle offered a choice of ale, beer, French, German, and Greek wines to drink. The food included beef, veal, lamb, bacon, capons, hens, plovers, woodcock, partridges, herons, snipe, leverets, rabbits, larks' tongues, oranges, pears, apples, pippins, quinces, prunes, raisins, almonds, dates, eight hundred eggs, ninety dishes of butter, eighty loaves of chestnut bread, three hundred wafers of marzipan and fifty pieces of gold leaf for gilding the gingerbread. As a menu it gives a fair idea of the type of food eaten at the time, though it makes no mention of venison, stewed sparrows, considered a great delicacy, or salads of artichokes, cabbage lettuces and cucumbers.

Henry was a tireless hunter of deer. A story is told of Henry getting lost while out hunting in the forest at Windsor. He finally made his way to Reading Abbey, where he passed himself off as a member of the King's Guard. The Abbot offered him hospitality as was customary in religious houses in those days. As Henry devoured a sirloin of beef with a hearty appetite the Abbot looked on wistfully and remarked that he would give one hundred pounds for such an appetite. Some weeks later the Abbot was horrified to find himself transported to London and clapped in the Tower, for no apparent reason. For a long time the terrified man was offered nothing but bread and water but one day a sirloin of beef was set before him, which he ate with gusto. Immediately Henry sprang out of the hiding place where he had been spying on the Abbot and demanded one hundred pounds for restoring his appetite to him, on pain of continued incarceration, saying, 'I have been your physician to cure you of your queasy stomach, and here, as I deserve, I demand my fee for the same.' The story is probably no more true than the one which credits Henry with having knighted a loin of beef he had enjoyed, thus creating the word sirloin, but it sums up the character of his youthful years.

✤

FORCED RABBIT WITH 'FINE SAUCE FOR A ROASTED RABBIT, USED TO KING HENRY THE EIGHTH'

The recipe for this sauce comes from *The Good Huswives Closet* published in 1591 in the reign of Henry's daughter Elizabeth I.

FOR THE FORCEMEAT:
225 g (½ lb) pig's liver
100 g (4 oz) butter
1 tablespoon fresh parsley, finely chopped
½ tablespoon fresh thyme, finely chopped
100g (4 oz) fresh white breadcrumbs
1 egg yolk
salt and pepper
50 ml (2 fl oz) approx. stock

Chop the liver and sauté in the butter. Mince finely. Combine the ingredients, season well and moisten with enough stock to make a fairly firm consistency.

FOR THE SAUCE:
1 large bunch parsley, finely chopped
65 g (2½ oz) butter
200 ml (8 fl oz) cider vinegar
50 ml (2 fl oz) water
100 g (4 oz) fresh white breadcrumbs
4 teaspoons castor sugar
salt and pepper

Stew the parsley gently in the butter for a few minutes. Add the vinegar and water and bring to the boil, stirring. Add the breadcrumbs and seasoning and stir well. Leave in a warm place for about 10 minutes while the breadcrumbs swell up. Beat the sauce thoroughly, adding a little more butter and water if it is too stiff. Reheat and serve. If reheating much later you will need to add more water as the bread will have become much stiffer.

1 cleaned, trussed rabbit	*1 glass red wine*
melted butter for basting	*250 ml (½ pint) stock made*
225 g (8 oz) streaky bacon rashers	*from the giblets*
1 tablespoon flour	*salt and pepper*

Stuff the rabbit with the forcemeat and sew up the opening. Place it in a flameproof roasting pan. Brush with melted butter and cover with the bacon rashers. Roast in a moderate oven, 190°C (375°F)/Gas 5 for about 1 hour, basting from time to time as rabbit tends to be rather dry. About 10 minutes before the rabbit is cooked remove the bacon to allow it to brown. When cooked transfer the rabbit to a warmed dish and keep hot.

Pour excess fat off meat juices. Add flour to pan and cook, scraping the pan, until the flour browns. Add wine and stock and bring to the boil, stirring. Keep stirring until the gravy thickens. Adjust seasoning, and serve the rabbit with the gravy, bread sauce and stuffing.

SERVES 4

✤

Peas and broccoli would be appropriate vegetables. If available begin with freshwater crayfish which were very popular at the time, otherwise use prawns. As a dessert serve *Codling Creame.* Codlings, or codlins were an old variety of cooking apple. About a pound of the apples should be boiled until pulpy with a little white wine and plenty of sugar. Make a custard with a pint of cream to three egg yolks. When the custard has thickened stir in the apple pulp. Stir until the custard has cooled slightly, then chill.

✤

EDWARD VI

(1547–1553)

✣ ✣

JUST TEN years old when he came to the throne, Edward, the son of Henry VIII by his third wife, Jane Seymour, was a studious little boy. His health was always delicate and he died only six years later. His last illness was not made any easier by his being pumped with arsenic which was considered to be a cure.

Edward was very serious and solemn for his age. He liked best to bury himself in his books and for someone so young his knowledge was impressive. He could speak Latin, French, Greek and Italian as well as his native English. He was an amateur astronomer and his main interest was theology. The usual activities of a boy of his age did not appeal to him. He even found the innocent fun and games enjoyed by his far from libertine sister, the future Queen Mary, rather too frivolous for his taste. Nevertheless it seems he did enjoy greatly the antics of George Ferrers, who was elected as Lord of Misrule, during the Christmas Season of 1552. The Lord of Misrule (another word for anarchy) was elected by lot to take charge of the festivities and organize the games and plays from Christmas Eve until Twelfth Night. He was totally in command, chose his own officers and at court even the monarch was expected to bow to his authority.

Inevitably people took advantage of Edward's youth and inexperience to exploit the situation and make what they could out of it. Edward tried very hard to maintain his position, although it was clear to outsiders that it was his two Protectors, Somerset and Northumberland, who were really in charge. One way of emphasizing the dignity and importance of the King was the ceremony that accompanied his every action. Edward had the rules of Assay kept rigidly even when he was not at court. This meant that all the elaborate ritual which accompanied the King's meals was carried out in the presence of an empty chair. Officers appeared at the table with dishes which were duly carved by the carver and checked for poison by the taster. All these personages paid appropriate obeisance to the absent monarch, even to the extent of walking away from the chair backwards. All of this was a very public affair, and most of the monarch's meals were eaten in public. A little later the strong-minded Elizabeth, when it was her turn to take the throne, rebelled against the lack of privacy and took to eating in a separate room, which was not received kindly by the rest of the court.

The standard of service, noticeably declining under Henry VIII, inevitably got worse under his son, who was unable to impose any real discipline. The servants had always been entitled to leftovers from any meal. Now they started taking the best bits before the meal was even served. In order to increase the booty, food was whisked away before it was scarcely begun. A poet at the time wrote,

> Slow be the sewers in serving in alway,
> But swift be they after, taking the meate away,
> A special custom is used them amonge,
> No dish to suffer on borde to be long.

RASPBERRY CREAM

Among the fruits which benefited from proper cultivation at this time was the raspberry, which had previously been more or less wild, a far cry from the luscious berry which we know today. As it improved with cultivation it became more popular, and it begins to be mentioned in recipe books. This typical recipe combines it with almonds which were as popular as ever. It shows how much more delicate and sophisticated some dishes now were, compared with their equivalents of a few hundred years previously.

250 ml (½ pint) single cream
250 ml (½ pint) double cream
1 blade of mace
100 g (4 oz) ground almonds

450 g (1 lb) fresh or frozen
*   raspberries*
37 g (1½ oz) approx. castor
*   sugar*

Bring the cream slowly to the boil in the top of a double saucepan with the mace and the ground almonds, stirring constantly with a wire whisk. When the cream has thickened remove from the heat and allow to cool.

Stew the raspberries with the sugar and a very little water until they are just soft. (About 5 minutes.) Frozen raspberries should be defrosted first and require no extra water. Allow to cool. Press through a sieve to remove the pips. Combine the raspberry pulp with the almond cream. Add more sugar if necessary. Serve chilled.

SERVES 8

✣

Mushrooms baked in the oven and basted with well-seasoned butter would make a good start to the meal. As a main course serve *Turkey Pie.* For this, cooked turkey is diced, seasoned with salt, nutmeg and cloves, moistened with a little stock from the giblets and baked under a puff pastry crust glazed with egg yolks.

✣

MARY I

(1553–1558)

✣ ✣

MARY WAS the first woman to reign over England in her own right. She had had a traumatic childhood, for Henry had divorced her mother, Catherine of Aragon, and mother and daughter were never able to feel secure again. At times they even feared for their lives. Mary is now best remembered for her fanatical anti-Protestantism which caused her to massacre a large number of her subjects. It is probable that she was never fully aware of the physical reality of what she was doing but was completely bound up in the theory of the whole controversy.

The cruelty for which she is remembered is in marked contrast to what we know of her character, for she seems to have been a gentle, homely woman who longed for the cosiness of a family life which was denied to her for much of her childhood and which she was never able to get from her own political marriage to Philip of Spain. After religion, which was her main obsession, she loved babies. She was frequently called upon to be a godparent and took her duties very seriously, usually presenting her godchild with a silver spoon which was a new custom fast becoming popular. She kept in touch with the other godmothers of these children, writing them letters in which she addressed them as 'My Good Gossip', the usual term by which fellow godmothers addressed each other at that time. In spite of the circumstances she was a loving elder sister to her brother Edward and sister Elizabeth while they were children, and was deeply hurt by Edward's later rejection of her as he came under the influence of some of his prim Protestant friends. Her great tragedy was that she never had any children of her own.

There are many accounts of what she looked like, mainly written by Spaniards who kept the Spanish court in touch with what was happening to her and her mother. We learn that she was never a beauty, although she had inherited a graceful way of carrying herself from her Spanish mother. She was also fond of expensive clothes and jewellery and presented a fashionable appearance because she always dressed in the Spanish style which was extremely popular at that time. As a child her hair had been blonde, but it darkened as she grew older. She had the rather vague expression which went with being short-sighted. Her colouring was considered her most attractive feature,

> Her couler comes and gose,
> With such a goodly grace,
> More ruddy than the rose,
> Within her lively face.

as one poetic admirer of the time put it. Her voice came as a surprise, being rather deep like a man's. Her laugh, too, was deep and throaty and she was inclined to laugh suddenly at something simple which amused her. Like the rest of the Tudors she was intelligent and well educated, and a first-class musician.

Food did not particularly interest her as she was too busy with her religious devotions and good works, often visiting the poor anonymously. The Venetian ambassador wrote, 'She is of very spare diet, and does not eat until one or two o'clock, although she rises at daybreak.' However we do know that she shared the royal partiality for lampreys and that she drank 'reyneshe wyne'.

✢

Almond Tart

In the sixteenth- and seventeenth-century recipe books there are often recipes for a pudding called Spanish Cream, or Spanish Pap. Presumably it has this name because anything fashionable and new was Spanish and vice versa. It is basically a custard made from cream and egg yolks, often thickened with a little rice flour and flavoured with orange flower water. The use of these flower waters, rose water and orange flower water in particular, became extremely popular at this time. Almond tart combines this popular flavour with another, almonds, which were being properly cultivated in England at this period.

225 g (8 oz) (flour weight) puff pastry	*4 tablespoons orange flower water*
100 g (4 oz) unsalted butter	*½ tablespoon castor sugar*
125 ml (¼ pint) single cream	*1 teaspoon ground nutmeg*
125 ml (¼ pint) double cream	*pinch salt*
100 g (4 oz) ground almonds	*3 egg yolks*

Line a 20 cm (8 in) flan tin with the pastry. Melt the butter in the cream gently, in the top of a double boiler. Add the almonds, orange flower water, sugar, nutmeg and salt. Heat a little longer until the mixture thickens. Leave to cool.

Beat the egg yolks together and beat them into the cooled almond cream. Pour into the prepared flan case and bake at 180°C (350°F)/Gas 4 until the filling sets. (About 45 minutes.) Sprinkle with castor sugar and serve, preferably while still warm.

Serves 6

✢

ELIZABETH I

(1558–1603)

✢ ✢

QUEEN ELIZABETH, who ruled England for over forty years, has become a legend. Her success as a monarch has made those who feel such success cannot be achieved by a woman, speculate that she may have been a man in disguise. This, they say, accounts for the fact that she never married. Others prefer to slander her image as the 'Virgin Queen', after whom the American state of Virginia was named, by saying she had affairs with many of her subjects, and with the Earl of Leicester in particular. She simply did what suited her and England, and did it with a great deal of charm, ignoring the opinions of others. Dithering until a problem sorted itself out without undue interference was a ploy which she used to perfection. One minister, driven to distraction, wrote 'the lack of a resolute answer from her Majesty, driveth me to the wall'.

Far from being masculine in appearance she was extremely attractive in her youth. From her father she had inherited a pale skin and red-blonde hair, which happened to be considered the epitome of beauty at the time. She was particularly proud of her slender white fingers and emphasized them with lots of rings. Painters, knowing which side their bread was buttered on, always made a feature of them in the many portraits of her. She was an impressive figure, taller than average, and very slim. She maintained her upright figure until she died, and remained sprightly even during old age by taking lots of exercise. She was particularly fond of hunting and hawking. As she got older her appearance became rather raddled. The beautiful red hair grew thin and Elizabeth took to wearing wigs of the same colour which were patently too young for her. Her beautiful skin became pockmarked after an attack of smallpox, and the face powder which she and other fashionable women used to heighten their pallor, contained arsenic, which eventually wrought havoc on the complexion. Her teeth blackened and fell out, causing her considerable pain, for there was no real dentistry to speak of, only a few quacks who resorted to pulling out any aching tooth, without the benefit of any sort of anaesthetic other than a very large dose of alcohol. Her partiality for sweet things, and soft white bread called manchet, accelerated the decay. Her godson and great favourite, Sir John Harrington, used to invent new sweetmeats to cheer her up if she felt a bit low. She would have done better to nibble a few nuts, known as 'shell fruit', which were being cultivated at the time. In spite of her raddled appearance in old age, poets and courtiers continued to flatter her and praise her beauty. Elizabeth was undoubtedly a sucker for any kind of flattery but her admirers during her later years were not necessarily hypocritical. The power of her personality was so great and her symbolic position as Queen and representative of England was so strong that she was a dazzling figure, and the fulsome praises of her were probably quite sincere.

Vanity and a love of show meant that Elizabeth loved clothes and dressing up. It took her about two hours to wash and dress in the morning. The elaborate dresses which she wears in her portraits were made specially for public occasions. In private she preferred to dress simply in black and white, which ironically caused her to stand out against the gaudiness of the rest of the court. She loved jewellery and had a large collection, much of it given by foreign ambassadors seeking to ingratiate themselves. On grand occasions she knew exactly how to dress for greatest effect. For her coronation she had four dresses. The first, for her procession through the city, was made of twenty-three yards of silver and gold cloth, with ermine trimmings and silver and gold lace. Her coronation robes included a vast cloak of ermine and embroidered silk, and during the ceremony she changed into two other dresses. Her stockings were of fine silk and gold thread. Her hat was of crimson velvet, decorated with gold and pearls.

Will-power seems to have been the dominating characteristic of Elizabeth's personality and she certainly knew how to get her own way. Harrington wrote, 'when she smiled, it was a pure sunshine, that everyone did choose to bask in if they could; but anon came a storm from a suddern gathering of clouds and the thunder fell in wondrous manner on all alike.' She was very careful with her money. Her household spent much of the time on the move from one large country house to another so that they were all fed at the expense of the Queen's hosts. Many of the large houses built during her reign were designed to accommodate the probable arrival of Elizabeth and her entourage. The savings Elizabeth made in this way were considerable, for household records still in existence show that the annual consumption of the royal household included sixty thousand pounds of butter; six hundred thousand gallons of beer; one thousand, two hundred and forty oxen; eight thousand, two hundred sheep; thirteen thousand, two hundred and sixty lambs; and four million, two hundred thousand eggs. The number of servants and private kitchens at court was on the increase, as people got into the habit of eating privately, in their own rooms. This added to Elizabeth's expenses as she was expected to feed the servants of her leading courtiers.

It may have been money worries that kept Elizabeth awake at night for she suffered from insomnia. She may also have been kept awake by the dubious smells emanating from the rather primitive plumbing. Elizabeth was immensely fastidious and very sensitive to bad smells, which frequently plagued her, surrounded as she was by a mass of unhygienic humanity. When annoyed, she swore, soundly and frequently, much to the annoyance of the Puritan faction. Her enjoyment of the theatre, (she was a patron of Shakespeare), also led to outbursts of Puritan disapproval. It was partly because of the need to keep her amused that traditional entertainments like dancing round the maypole still thrived in the towns and villages she visited. Elizabeth did not take too much notice of Puritan disapproval of these harmless activities: she knew her people loved seeing her and entertaining her. She was loved by all her subjects, however lowly, for she had a knack for getting on with people. This may have been partly a result of her genuine interest in them and her realization that her strength lay in the loyalty and affection of her people.

London was a rich, thriving metropolis, and while the Queen was in town, life was an endless series of entertainments and banquets given by rich noblemen and merchants. It was now the custom for the court to spend Christmas at Whitehall and not at Gloucester. Elizabeth encouraged the revival of traditional entertainment at Christmas, and throughout the year. On 17 November, the anniversary of her accession to the throne, medieval tilts were held. These imitations of the old jousts, and the ideas of courtesy and chivalry which they re-awakened, were good for Elizabeth's image as a beautiful woman for whom her subjects were prepared to fight; and the colourful spectacle was enjoyed by all types of people.

Although she attended many banquets and entertainments,

the Queen preferred whenever possible to eat in private, unseen by anyone except a few of her ladies. Privacy was one luxury which a monarch was expected to do without, and so this custom was rather disapproved of. As a concession, Sunday was a day on which she was served in public, with all the attendant ceremonial, watched by interested visitors. Even so, she actually *ate* the food in private. Another luxury which was not for the monarch was hot food. By the time the food had been decorated, carried miles from the kitchens and then stood on the table while the ceremonial was performed, it was stone cold. When the Queen was at Windsor Castle the food was not even cooked in the castle kitchens but brought from a public oven about half a mile away.

Elizabeth was no glutton and only ate when she was hungry. She observed all the days of fast and abstinence. Her preference was for lighter food and for poultry rather than red meat; thirty-three thousand chickens were eaten by her household every year. She liked to eat very simple food, plain meats and salads. Nor was she a great drinker. Apparently she drank her wine well watered-down, and she particularly disliked the old strong beer, called March ale because it was brewed in that month. Wherever she went she insisted that the beer should be light and freshly brewed. Her sweet tooth meant she had a passion for cakes, made with lots of sugar and currants. In this she was typical of all her people. The English were, and still are, known for eating sweet things. During Elizabeth's reign England imported nearly all the currants available. Potatoes were introduced at this time, and so were tomatoes. However these last were considered poisonous and for a long time were only used as a decoration. Asparagus also became popular and so did capers. Boiled mutton and caper sauce was soon a standard English favourite.

✢

PORK AND PEASE

There is a story that in 1554 when Elizabeth was released from a spell in the Tower of London by her sister, Queen Mary, she went to give thanks for her deliverance at the Church of All Hallows. While the bells were still pealing in celebration she went round the corner to an inn, then known as the King's Head, where she ate a meal of pork with pease pudding. With the generous tip which she had given him, the parish clerk instituted an annual pork and pease dinner at his house, as a reminder of the event.

1 bacon joint, about 1.35 kg (3 lb)	*2 egg yolks*
	1 tablespoon sugar
FOR THE PUDDING:	*salt and pepper*
450 g (1 lb) dried green peas	*1 onion, sliced*
2 teaspoons fresh parsley, chopped	*1 carrot, sliced*
4 teaspoons fresh mint, chopped	*1 parsnip, sliced*
50 g (2 oz) butter	*2 teaspoons sugar*

Soak the bacon in cold water overnight. Leave the peas to soak overnight in cold water.

Boil the peas with the herbs until really soft. (About 2 hours.) Drain, press through a sieve, or purée in a blender. Beat the butter, egg yolks, sugar and seasoning into the peas. Either pack the mixture into a well-greased pudding basin, cover tightly with foil and boil in a large saucepan for 1 hour, or wring out a cotton cloth in boiling water, dredge it thoroughly with flour, and spoon the pudding mixture on to the cloth. Tie the ends of the cloth securely and put the pudding in with the bacon, hanging it over the edge of the saucepan, for the last hour of cooking. If using this method, which is the original one, be sure not to let the water go off the boil.

The bacon should be covered with water in a pan and brought slowly to the boil with the sliced vegetables and sugar. Simmer gently until tender. (About 1½–2 hours).

Serve slices of the bacon with the pudding and a spoonful or two of the stock. Reserve the rest of the stock for soup, as cooks most certainly would have done at the time.

SERVES 4

~THE STUARTS~

JAMES I

(1603–1625)

✢ ✢

JAMES COULD not have been more different from the well-loved Elizabeth who preceded him. Where she was elegant, he was slovenly; where she showed genuine interest in her subjects, he chose to avoid them like the plague; where she was adored, he was disliked. He consequently went in constant fear of assassination, and several people observed that he wore heavily quilted doublets to prevent a stiletto from reaching his heart. These doublets unfortunately emphasized his skinny legs.

Of course, being a Scot, he was at a disadvantage to begin with, for the insular English were only too ready to find fault. Polite court ladies wrote home deploring the deterioration of the court since the arrival of the Scots, attributing to their arrival, for example, the fact that they were now all lice-ridden.

James was intelligent, well read and well educated, though he was perhaps not as great an intellectual as he himself believed. He was an eminent theologian, and during his reign the Authorized Version of the Bible was made. He liked to be best at everything, even the length of time he could go without sleep, retiring in a sulk if he was outclassed. A contemporary, admittedly somewhat biased against him, wrote,

> His beard was very thin: his tongue too large for his mouth, which ever made him speak full in the mouth, and made him drink very uncomely, as if eating his drink, which came out into the cup of each side of his mouth; his skin was as soft as taffeta sarsnet, which felt so because hee never washt his hands, onely rubb'd his fingers ends slightly with the wet end of a napkin... his walke was ever circular, his finger ever in that walke fidling about his cod piece.

With James it was usually less a question of what he positively liked as what he disliked least. He did show a real passion for hunting, sometimes, in spite of his feeble body, staying in the saddle for six hours at a time and then sitting out in the cold wind drinking, so that he was always catching colds. However, he could not bear the fashionable side of court life, the dancing, the flirting, the extravagant clothes and particularly the fashion for wearing ear rings.

When it came to food he did know that he positively disliked pork in any form. Sir Walter Scott, who felt he had an intimate knowledge of James, wrote that 'James's own proposed banquet for the Devil was a loin of pork, a poll of ling, with a pipe of tobacco for digestion.' To amuse the court Sir George Goring once brought to a party '4 brawny pigs, piping hot, bitted and harnessed with ropes of sausages, all tied to a monstrous pudding'. On another occasion a piglet was dressed like a baby and a mock christening was performed. It may have amused the courtiers but it revolted James. The King was also revolted by the newly introduced custom of smoking tobacco which he called 'this precious stink'. He brought his intellectual powers to bear on the subject in the treatise entitled *Counterblaste to Tobacco*. A short extract gives a good idea of the tone in which it was written.

And for the vanities committed in this filthy custom, is it not both great vanity and uncleanness, that at the table, a place of respect, of cleanliness, of modesty, men should not be ashamed, to sit tossing tobacco pipes and puffing of the smoke of tobacco one to another, making the filthy smoke and stink therof, to exhale athwart the dishes, and infect the air, when very often men that abhor it are at their repast.

It seems that if he liked anything at all it was a few of his native Scottish dishes, and fresh fruit. He crammed himself with vast quantities of grapes, cherries and strawberries and was constantly suffering from an upset stomach. It is surprising that he was not more interested in what he ate, as the cooking in Scotland at the time was very good. James's grandmother, the mother of Mary Queen of Scots, had been French and had brought lots of French ideas with her to Scotland. French cookery was undergoing a period of change from the almost universal medieval type of food, to something more like the sort of style we associate with France today. This was partly a result of the Italian influence on France, as many Italian cooks had gone to the French court with Catherine de Medici. It is one of these cooks who is credited with the invention of ice-cream.

Though he was not much interested in the food, James did revel in the entertainment which came after. Gambling he loved, and masques and pageants. A love of theatre was one of the few things he had in common with his wife, Anne of Denmark. Inigo Jones frequently designed the sets and costumes for these elaborate entertainments, though not to the satisfaction of one person at least. Ben Jonson, who wrote many of the masques, remarked disparagingly that Jones 'should return to his oulde trade of bricklaying again'. These masques often followed dinner served in the newly fashionable form of a double supper or ante-supper. An elaborate supper would be set out with the choicest and most expensive dishes to greet the guests on their arrival. When they had admired its appearance sufficiently it was removed uneaten and the table piled high with a completely fresh supper which could be eaten as well as admired. This waste and gross overeating was put down to Scottish influence by the English.

James's disgusting behaviour and that of his sycophants seems to have come to a head during the visit of the King of Denmark, Christian IV, a notorious sot. There was a quite unparalleled orgy of drunkenness lasting for days, with men and women rolling about on the floor, totally inebriated. Ladies representing virtues such as Peace, Victory, Faith and Hope in a symbolic pageant for their majesties' entertainment, were unable to get through their duties for 'wine did so occupy their upper chambers'. Hope and Faith were forced to beat a hasty retreat and they were found by Charity 'sick and spewing in the lower hall'. The lady playing the Queen of Sheba, so blind drunk that she did not see the steps as she brought her offerings to the Danish King, tripped, and landed all the wine, cream and jelly in his lap. Fortunately he was too far gone to care, but rising unsteadily in order to dance with her, he passed out and had to be carried to bed still covered with the remains of the food. This and similar incidents disgusted those who were sober, for they felt it was the epitome of what they had expected from their new Scottish King, and his extravagant and intemperate friends.

FRIAR'S CHICKEN

According to Sir Walter Scott this was a favourite of James I. It is a nourishing, easily digested soup, which would have been very soothing for a man constantly troubled by stomach-ache.

900 g (2 lb) knuckle of veal
1 young chicken, skinned and
   jointed or 4 large chicken joints,
   skinned
1 level teaspoon ground cinnamon

salt and white pepper
1 tablespoon fresh parsley,
   chopped
3 eggs, beaten
parsley to serve

Place the veal in a large saucepan, cover with water, boil for 2 hours. Strain. Add the chicken and cinnamon to the resulting stock, and season strongly with salt and pepper. Simmer for 10 minutes, add the parsley. Continue cooking until the chicken is tender. (About 20 minutes more.) When the chicken is tender allow it to cool, remove the flesh from the bones and cut it into bite-sized pieces. Reheat the broth with the chicken. Remove from the heat and beat in the eggs. Reheat without boiling. Check seasoning, and serve sprinkled with fresh parsley. Add extra eggs if you like a thicker soup.

SERVES 4–6

✧

ATHOLE BROSE

'Brose' comes from the French. It means the dish contains oatmeal steeped in water. *Athole Brose is* a traditional Scottish recipe.

100 g (4 oz) finely ground oatmeal
125 ml (¼ pint) water
50 ml (2 fl oz) whisky

2 tablespoons clear, heather honey
125 ml (¼ pint) single cream
125 ml (¼ pint) double cream

Mix the oatmeal with the water and leave to stand for about 30 minutes. Press the mixture through a fine sieve to extract all the liquid. Stir in the whisky and dissolve the honey in the liquid. Beat the cream until stiff but smooth. Gradually add the whisky-flavoured brose. Spoon into 6 separate serving dishes and serve chilled, topped with a few toasted oatflakes. Do not leave in the refrigerator for too long or the mixture will begin to separate.

SERVES 6

✧

CHARLES I

(1625–1649)

✢ ✢

CHARLES I made a poor job of being King and was eventually executed, gaining more respect for the way in which he faced his death than he ever seems to have received during his life. He was regarded by many as a martyr who died for the sake of the Anglican Church, for politics and religion were inextricably bound up with one another. Relics of his death were sold rather like relics of the martyrs of the Roman Empire. They included the handkerchief he used, with the stains from his blood.

Charles's court had shown a marked reaction against the slovenliness of his father's. There was no drunken revelry but everything became extremely formal and reflected Charles's own very high-flown ideas of the uniqueness and importance of the monarch. The King was served at table by people on their knees, a custom which was dying out in the rest of Europe. The mutual devotion of Charles and his French Queen, Henrietta Maria, was another marked change from what people had come to expect from the court. The family was a close one, and their interests were cultured rather than bawdy. They enjoyed theatre, music and painting. Much fine painting was done in England at the time, mainly because there were many rich people commissioning family portraits. Van Dyck came to England and painted many, now famous, portraits of the Royal Family and their court. Inigo Jones was at the height of his powers, and in 1630 he built Covent Garden Market for the Earl of Bedford. It was not only important architecturally but an indication of the increasing sale of fresh produce in the town and the growth of the market gardening industry to cope with it.

Cookery flourished and there was a glut of cookery books where formerly there had been a shortage. One, *The Queen's Closet Opened*, was supposed to contain the recipes of Henrietta Maria herself, although by the time it was published she was in exile in France. It gives a good idea of what constituted English cookery before the influence of French cooking which predominated in the wealthy households after Charles II returned from exile in France. It included the inevitable household hints and medical advice as well as recipes. Another of these cookery and household advice books was one by Sir Kenelm Digby, who had been in charge of Henrietta Maria's household, and who had followed the Stuarts into exile. His book has many recipes eaten by the Royal Family, with names like *The Queen Mother's Hotchpot of Mutton* and *The Queen's Morning Broth*.

From all these cookery books it appears that the English loved pies and salads. Later there were complete books dedicated to the subject of salads. As for pies, the author of a cookery book called *The Perfect Cook* based largely on the French cuisine, apologized for having the nerve to give instructions 'To this Nation, where every young matron and damsel are so well vers'd in the pastry art, so that they may out vie the best Forreign Pastry cooks in all the world besides'.

It was at this period that there was a fashion for enclosing live creatures under a pastry crust, in order to give the guests an amusing surprise. An Italian called Epulario published a cookery book, translated into English in 1598, which contained a recipe for a pie of live birds. Such recipes gave rise to the nursery rhyme:

> Sing a song of sixpence a pocket full of rye,
> Four-and-twenty blackbirds baked in a pie,
> When the pie was opened the birds began to sing,
> Oh, wasn't that a dainty dish to set before a king.

Unfortunately tuneful blackbirds were not the only animals to be encased in a pie. Robert May was a Master Chef at court during the first half of the seventeenth century, cooking for Charles I, as well as his father. In 1664 he published a book called *The Accomplisht Chef*, in which he recalled the sort of cooking he did, a form of cooking which was already going out of fashion as he wrote about it. He describes some of the strange dishes he concocted for the delight of the court and among them are pies,

  where lifting first the lid offone pye, out skip some frogs; which make the Ladies to skip and shriek; next after the other pye, whence come out the birds, who by a natural instinct flying in the light, will put out the candles, so that what with the flying birds and skipping Frogs, the one above, the other beneath, will cause much delight and pleasure to the whole company.

The strangest occasion of all was when a pie crust was cut and out jumped a dwarf, wearing a suit of armour. This was Jeffrey Hudson, the smallest of the King's dwarfs, who was well under two feet tall. The King and Queen were both very fond of dwarfs and there were several at court. Jeffrey Hudson had come as a gift from the Duke and Duchess of Buckingham. He was so small that one of the King's largest porters would carry him around in his pocket and keep the court amused by putting him between two pieces of bread and pretending to eat him like a sandwich.

✤

CHERRY PIE

Some form of cherry pie was a popular dish with many of the kings and queens of England from Queen Elizabeth to Queen Victoria, who liked cherry tart with lots of cream. This version is a typical seventeenth-century fruit pie in which the juice is thickened with egg yolks, which make it extremely rich.

900 g (2 lb) stoned morello cherries (bottled ones are excellent)
½ litre (1 pint) red wine or 375 ml (¾ pint) red wine and 125 ml (¼ pint) of juice from bottled cherries
2 egg yolks, beaten

175 g (6 oz) castor sugar, a little less if using bottled fruit
¼ teaspoon ground ginger
½ teaspoon ground cinnamon
225 g (8 oz) (flour weight) puff pastry
a little castor sugar for the crust

Cook the cherries in the wine, sugar and spices until the fruit is tender and the liquid has reduced to about 250 ml (½ pint). If using bottled fruit reduce the syrup to about 250 ml (½ pint) before adding the cherries, which will need very little cooking.

Drain the cherries and place in a pie dish. Beat the egg yolks into the wine syrup and pour over the fruit. Place a pie funnel in the centre of the dish.

Roll out the pastry and cut a strip about 1 cm (½ in) wide to line the rim of the pie dish. Moisten the pastry strip with a little rose water or plain water and place the pie crust on it. Seal the edges by pinching them together. If not using a pie funnel cut three diagonal slits in the centre of the crust to allow the steam to escape. Bake in a preheated hot oven 220°C (425°F)/Gas 7 until cooked. (About 30 minutes.) Sprinkle with castor sugar and serve hot or cold.

SERVES 8

JOSEPH COOPER'S RECEIPT TO FRY ARTICHOKES

Boyl and sever all from the Bottoms, and slice them in the midst, and quarter it, dip them in Batter and fry them in Butter, for the Sauce take Butter and Sugar with the juice of an Orange. Dish your Artichokes with this sauce (being fried brown) and lay boyl'd marrow of bones on them. Garnish it with Orange and serve up.

✥

As a main course serve Dover Sole, poached for 20 minutes in a little melted butter and claret and garnished with slices of lemon and orange. As a side dish salad could be served. Salad was by now a fine art and often a meal in itself. John Evelyn, the diarist, wrote a book in 1699 entirely on the subject of salads. In it he recommends seventy-three possible herbs or vegetables, and advises a light hand with the garlic. 'To be sure, tis not for Ladies Palats, nor those who court them, farther than to permit a light touch on the Dish with a Clove thereof, …'

This is a salad made by Robert May, the Master chef at Charles I's court. It makes an interesting contrast to King Richard II's salad, in *The Forme of Cury*. (See page 53).

✥

ROBERT MAY'S SALAD

Take all manner of knots of buds of sallet herbs, buds of pot-herbs, or any green herbs, as sage, mint, balm, burnet, violet-leaves, red coleworts streaked of divers fine colours, lettice, any flowers, blanched almonds, blue figs, raisins of the sun, currans, capers, olives; then dish the sallet in a heap or pile, being mixed with some of the fruits, and all finely washed and swung in a napkin, then about the centre lay first sliced figs, next capers, and currans then almonds and raisins, next olives, and lastly either jagged beats, jagged lemons, jagged cucumbers, or cabbidge lettice in quarters, good oyl and wine vinegar, sugar or none.

CHARLES II

(1660–1685)

✤ ✤

CHARLES II is better remembered for his mistresses and his extravagant living, than for his statesmanship, although he was no fool and managed his reign rather better than many others. He was not good-looking in the conventional sense, but he was tall, with shiny black hair, twinkling eyes and a great deal of smooth charm. He did not like to refuse anyone anything outright, feeling it would be bad for his generous image. He therefore took to walking about his palace very fast so that no-one could get hold of him and ask him for favours. His court, which he modelled on that of his cousin, Louis XIV of France, was famous for its 'inexpressible luxury'. Yet after eleven years of Puritan repression under Oliver Cromwell, the people were more than ready to give the 'Merry Monarch' a hero's welcome, and to turn a blind eye to his excesses.

His wife, Catherine of Braganza, was a meek and mousy little woman, who had little to do with court life and even less to do with politics. 'They have brought me a bat instead of a woman,' Charles is said to have cried, on first being introduced to her. Although he was never deliberately unkind to her, Charles neglected her shamefully, preferring his mistresses, who could certainly not have been called meek. Nell Gwynne, the little orange seller, seems to have been particularly raucous and able to look after herself. On one occasion when Charles was visiting her and their small son she yelled across the room to the boy, 'Come here you little bastard.' The King was deeply hurt to hear his son being addressed so coarsely and remonstrated with Nell. She pointed out that the child really did not have a proper name. So Charles immediately gave him the title of Duke of St Albans and Nell was able to congratulate herself on a ploy which had secured a good rank and title for her son. Nell Gwynne's character must have suited Charles rather well, for the general opinion was that Charles was motivated by earthy rather than sentimental considerations when it came to his love affairs. However, he did on at least one occasion turn to poetry, writing verses with the refrain 'There's no hell like loving too well.'

Charles, having returned from exile in France, and anxious to rebuild the strength and glamour of the monarchy, decided to restore the importance of some of the old institutions. He took a particular interest in the Order of the Garter, which had rather declined in importance. Great feasts, reminiscent of the medieval occasions, were held at Windsor Castle for the King and his knights. The menu for one of these feasts gives us an idea of the variety of food available at the time. Among the items served were oysters, lobsters, scallops, prawns, cockles, caviare, mussels, shellfish bisque, wildboar pie, umble pie, turkey, rabbit, chicken, lamprey pie, pigeon pie, a great deal of 'sallet', and cold 'sparagrass' (asparagus). The total cost of the feast was £2,394 17s 8½d. This was an incredible amount of money and Charles must have been quite disappointed when his noble knights treated the whole occasion quite literally as an enormous bun fight, and ended up throwing the food at each other and at the spectators in the gallery. Not that he was really in a position to be too critical for it was known that the King was often so drunk that he was in 'a maudlin pickle'.

The return of Charles from exile in France created a whole new fashion in things French. The court of the 'Sun King', Louis XIV, was undoubtedly the cultural and fashion centre of Europe and the English court followed its lead slavishly. It was not only clothes, hair and architecture which were affected: cooking, too, was changed by the French influence. It sounded the final death knell for the strong flavours of medieval food so heavily spiced that the flavour of the meat or fish was not noticeable. Wealthy English households would send their chefs to France for instruction in the French methods. Those who could not afford such luxury all the time could hire a freelance chef, as Samuel Pepys sometimes did. The most famous French chef of the time was Varenne, who wrote a book called *Le Pastissier François*. In it many of the basics of modern haute cuisine appear for the first time. By this time it was considered 'comely and decent' to use a fork but many people still did not bother. In *The Whole Body of Cookery Dissected*, published in 1661, a year after Charles returned from France, the author, Will Rabisha, included carving instructions from the 1508 *Boke of Kervynge*, which were based on the assumption that people eat with their fingers off bread trenchers.

Along with new cooking methods there were new foods to experiment with. In 1664 pineapples receive their first mention. They were so expensive that they were often used simply as decoration and they became a symbol of generous hospitality: it is for this reason that they often occur as decoration on gate posts or above an entrance. Tea was sold publicly for the first time in England and was immediately condemned by writers and clergymen as being dangerous to health and morals. Oranges were still a great luxury, although they had been known in England since the thirteenth century. They initially came from the East and were later grown in Spain. England's constant wars with Spain had prevented them from becoming commonplace. As the food changed, so did the drink. Brandy, a French drink, was beginning to find favour with the upper classes, though most people distilled their own *aqua vitae* at home, from whatever fruit was available. Champagne, too, was introduced, though it was not to become synonymous with luxury for some time.

✤

WHYPT SULLIBUB

Syllabub was originally made 'under the cow'. That is, the wine and sugar would be placed in a basin and the cow milked directly into the wine, to produce a frothy and refreshing drink. Later syllabub became a little more varied and generally more solid, so that it was eaten with a spoon and not drunk. Charles II was extremely fond of syllabub and kept a few cows in St James's Park, so that he could have fresh syllabub whenever he felt like it. A whipped syllabub is the nearest we can get to that drink these days.

¼ teaspoon ground nutmeg	2 egg whites
1 piece lemon peel	37 g (1½ oz) castor sugar
250 ml (½ pint) sweet white wine	
250 ml (½ pint) double cream	FOR THE BASE:
50 ml (2 fl oz) sherry	275 ml (6 fl oz) wine
1 teaspoon orange flower water	50 ml (2 fl oz) milk

Leave the nutmeg and lemon peel to steep in the wine overnight. Strain the wine and add it to the cream with the sherry and orange flower water. Whip the egg whites and sugar together until stiff. Fold into the cream and continue whipping with a wire whisk.

Combine the milk and wine for the base and pour a little into six glasses. As you whip the cream and wine mixture, spoon the resulting froth on to the wine base as you go along. Serve as soon as possible because the foam will eventually subside.

SERVES 6

✤

JAMES II

(1685–1688)

✥ ✥

CHARLES II had had plenty of illegitimate children, but unfortunately no legitimate ones and the throne was inherited by his brother. James completely lacked Charles's sense of politics and the art of the possible. He did not know how to compromise, although Charles had forever been trying to teach him. It meant that he was publicly a staunch Roman Catholic, with a Roman Catholic foreign policy and a Roman Catholic wife, even a Roman Catholic heir to the throne, at just the period in history when everything 'Popish' was anathema to all good Englishmen. Parliament therefore invited his Protestant daughter by his first marriage and her Protestant husband, William of Orange, to come and take over, and James was forced to abdicate.

He seems to have been a courageous, talented and hard-working man, and he worked loyally on his brother's behalf. It was while he was acting as Charles's Lord High Commissioner in Scotland that his wife, Mary of Modena, is said to have introduced tea to the Scots. Apparently it was not an immediate success and was despised as being very much a woman's drink. In spite of James's obsession with his religion he was a libertine and a womaniser. But he was so dull and pompous with it that people could not bring themselves to look on his indiscretions with the same amused tolerance they had shown Charles II's exploits. He committed the unforgivable sin of lacking any sense of humour. Since he personally was abstemious he cracked down on the amount of drinking at court, which did nothing to increase his popularity. When James taxed Charles II with endangering his own life by walking in the park unattended by any sort of guard Charles, who was *not* lacking in humour, was able to reply, 'No kind of danger James, for I'm sure no man in England will take away my life to make you King.'

During James's reign the First Master Chef of the King's Kitchen was Patrick Lambe, who had begun his working life as a 'child of the pastry' in the kitchens of Charles II. He put into practice the precepts of the new-style French chefs, and when he retired, in the reign of Queen Anne, he published a book called *Royal Cookery or the Complete Court Cook*.

✦

SALMON IN CHAMPAIGN WINE

James's rigid Catholicism meant he would have had many fish days to observe. *Salmon in Champaign* is an ideal dish with which to fast, for the renunciation involved cannot be considered very great. It is a dish from the book of Patrick Lambe, the court's Master Chef, and it shows clearly how much cooking had changed from the days when sturgeon was served with a simple parsley and vinegar sauce. In his enormous kitchens a chef like Patrick Lambe would have had vast amounts of stock and of cullis, a greatly reduced rich stock, used for thickening sauces. The original recipe specifies a crayfish cullis for thickening the champagne sauce, as well as white breadcrumbs. These have been replaced by the modern method of thickening using a roux of flour and butter.

The original recipe calls for a whole salmon but this has been adapted to a smaller amount sufficient for four people. The amount of champagne required for this recipe is exactly one bottle. A light white wine makes an acceptable substitute.

1.2 kg (2¹/₂ lb) middle cut fresh salmon

FOR THE COURT BOUILLON:
1 litre (2 pints) water
250 ml (1 pint) champagne
1 tablespoon fresh parsley, chopped
1 bouquet garni
1 bay leaf
1 teaspoon black peppercorns
1 teaspoon salt

FOR THE SAUCE:
20 g (³/₄ oz) unsalted butter
20 g (³/₄ oz) cornflour
250 ml (¹/₂ pint) cream (¹/₂ single, ¹/₂ double)
25 g (1 oz) unsalted butter
100 g (4 oz) white button mushrooms, sliced
200 ml (8 fl oz) champagne
salt

Place all the ingredients for the court bouillon in a saucepan and simmer gently for 30 minutes. Strain. Poach the fish gently in the court bouillon for about 35 minutes. The fish should come away easily from the bone when tested with a skewer. Drain. Serve with champagne sauce.

To make the sauce, first melt 20 g (¾ oz) butter gently in a saucepan, then add the cornflour and mix thoroughly to make a roux. Gradually add the cream, stirring all the time, to make a smooth sauce. Melt 25 g (1 oz) butter. Add the sliced mushrooms and cook them gently for about 2 minutes. Remove from the heat. Add the wine, return to the heat and boil rapidly until the liquid is reduced by about half. Allow to cool slightly. Gradually add the cream sauce to the wine and mushrooms so that you get a sauce which is about the consistency of thick cream. It may not require the entire 250 ml (½ pint) of cream sauce to do this. Reheat gently without boiling, add a very little salt to bring out the flavour and serve with the salmon.

SERVES 4

WILLIAM & MARY

(1689–1702 & 1694)

✦ ✦

JAMES II'S daughter Mary, and her husband and cousin William of Orange, were joint rulers of England, 'Williamnmary' as they have been known to generations of schoolchildren. Mary was charming and popular, William was dour and unattractive. Mary was devoted to William; William thought he could do without Mary, and for a long time had an ageing mistress. Yet when Mary died of smallpox aged only thirty-two William found he was almost inconsolable and turned to drink.

Mary II was a natural homemaker, with a gift for making even the cumbersome and draughty royal residences seem cosy. The eleven years of domestic contentment she had spent in Holland, before she returned to England in rather upsetting circumstances, remained her happiest memory, and she did her best to recreate those days in her new home. For a long time after they arrived in England shiploads of their personal possessions were sent over from Holland. The blue and white Delft china Mary was so fond of was imported, and she introduced her favourite pets, pug dogs, into this country, for she needed something to lavish her affection on. William was forever off on his campaigns and they had no children, which was a constant source of sadness to them both.

William III was admired for his courage and endurance. He was always in the thick of any battle, a continual source of anxiety for his loving wife, and he never asked his soldiers to do what he would not do himself. He lived rough when on campaigns, even though he was not physically strong and suffered badly from asthma. But though William was admired for his sterling qualities he was not loved as Mary was by her people. Mary had a warm and attractive personality and a great sense of humour. A rhyme of the time goes:

> King James's disobedient daughter,
> Who was addicted very much to laughter,
> And lived as if there was no world hereafter.

She took little interest in running the country, except when William was away. One of her greatest pleasures was a good gossip about the latest court scandal. She enjoyed rich clothes and jewels and ran up enormous dress bills because she knew William liked to see her fashionably and richly dressed. While in Holland she had been considered the absolute epitome of fashion and style. At the same time she was conscious of the great deficiencies in her education and was always reading in an attempt to improve herself. She was fond of natural history and also read novels, which were a comparatively new form of literature, not totally acceptable because the word was associated with French romances of a slightly florid nature.

We know a great deal about William and Mary's household because right at the beginning of their reign instructions for its organization and day-to-day running were set out in a document entitled *The Establishment: The Yearly charge of their Majesties Dyet, with incidents for Housekeeping*. This was signed by William himself and he clearly had no intention whatsoever of being embezzled by his household staff. Details of expenditure go right down to the last royal candle. Perhaps that is not really surprising as the cost of lighting the royal palaces was almost twice the cost of the food. It was a traditional servant's 'perk' to have the candle stubs at the end of every day and a careful estimate of the number required in the year helped to cut down on fiddles like putting in fresh candles just before the household retired.

Royal menus were carefully regulated as well. At dinner ten meat dishes were to be served to the King and Queen, at supper there were eight. There was also provision for seasonal delicacies like green peas. On one occasion when Mary's sister, Princess Anne, was dining with them William was so bored that he became totally detached from what was going on, a common habit with him, and mechanically ate a whole dish of peas which happened to be placed in front of him. Anne was particularly upset, not just because she had been ignored – she probably had not even noticed for William would often go through an entire meal without uttering a word – but because she was particularly fond of peas herself.

The royal pair did not drink anything overly exotic, but generally drank claret and the Rhenish wine of which the first Queen Mary had been fond. Both of them liked the newly fashionable drink of hot chocolate, and drank it for breakfast at the newly fashionable hour of nine o'clock, accompanied by fresh rolls and Dutch butter imported specially for them. It can be assumed that in general they ate very well as the Master Chef continued to be Patrick Lambe, who had served Mary's father and uncle.

ROAST MUTTON WITH ANCHOVY SAUCE

Roast mutton featured frequently on William and Mary's table. The addition of anchovies to the sauce was not uncommon at this time for their strong flavour helped to mask any taint in the meat.

*1 shoulder of mutton, 1.35-1.8 kg
(3-4 lb) (lamb can be substituted but does not have the
same strong flavour)
2 anchovies, finely chopped
1 onion, finely chopped*

*125 ml (5 fl oz) hot water
200 ml (8 fl oz) port
salt and white pepper
175 g (6 oz) fresh white
breadcrumbs
50 g (2 oz) butter*

Season the mutton well and place on a wire rack in a flameproof roasting dish. Roast at 190°C (375°F)/Gas 5 for 20 minutes per 450 g (1 lb) – about 1 hour 20 minutes.

When the meat has been cooking for about 1 hour, remove it from the oven. Transfer the meat, on the rack, to a dish and keep hot. Pour excess fat off the meat juices in the roasting dish. Add the anchovy, onion, water and 150 ml (6 fl oz) port to the dish. Bring to the boil on top of the stove and simmer until the onion is tender. (About 10 minutes.)

Return the meat, on the rack, to the roasting dish and continue cooking in the oven until done. Baste the meat frequently with the anchovy sauce.

When the meat is cooked transfer it to a heated serving dish and keep hot. Pour excess fat off the meat juices in the roasting dish, add the remaining 50 ml (2 fl oz) port and reheat the sauce on top of the stove, scraping round the pan to include all the meat juices. Season the sauce to taste with salt and pepper.

Fry the breadcrumbs lightly in the butter. Season with salt and pepper and sprinkle thickly over the meat on the serving dish. Serve the meat with the sauce separately.

✣

ANNE

(1702–1714)

✢ ✢

QUEEN ANNE herself was not terribly interesting. She was more interested in domestic matters than politics. During her reign England was united with Scotland; the Duke of Marlborough won the Battles of Blenheim, Ramillies and Malplaquet; the General Post Office was established; and the first daily newspaper went into circulation.

Queen Anne's concept of the importance of the monarchy led to a great deal of finicky protocol which the Queen insisted should be observed down to the last detail. In spite of this she is the last English monarch to have eaten with her fingers. Much of the really fashionable entertaining went on in the houses of Anne's wealthiest subjects. One such wealthy hostess was the Queen's friend and confidante, Sarah, Duchess of Marlborough. Anne and Sarah wrote to each other using pseudonyms: Sarah was Mrs Freeman and Anne was Mrs Morley. But Sarah eventually overstepped the mark and their curious intimacy came to an end. Anne transferred her affections to another friend, Lady Masham. Anne's need for friendship may have been due to the inadequacies of her husband, George of Denmark, with whom she had an amicable but not particularly close relationship. If Anne was dull, George was duller. He completely ignored politics, being more interested in gardening and also drink. His wife's uncle, Charles II, who was quickly bored by tedious people, called him 'a great jar or vessel standing still and receiving unmoved and undisturbed so much liquor whenever it came to his turn'. Unfortunately drink did not make him a brighter companion. Charles remarked despairingly, 'I've tried him drunk and I've tried him sober and there's nothing in him.'

It may be that Anne found him more tolerable drunk, for a rumour went about that she consoled herself for the tedium of her life by sipping 'cold tea' from a porcelain cup, the 'tea' being brandy. She and George had more than a dozen children, none of whom survived, and it is not surprising that this took its toll on her appearance. She certainly became very fat and blotchy, which provoked other rumours of secret gin drinking, maybe because gin was popularly supposed to be good for 'women's ailments'. There was probably no truth in the rumours at all, but as Anne grew older being overweight became such a problem for her that, like her ancestor Henry VIII, she needed a complicated system of ropes and pullies to get her upstairs. Her father, James II, had been a keen horseman, and had popularized fox hunting for the aristocracy, as deer became rather thin on the ground due to the aristocracy's previous efforts and the contraction of the forested areas. Anne took after James in her love of horses. She loved both horse racing and fox hunting but her weight made riding impossible. Instead she 'drove to hounds' in a carriage, epitomizing Oscar Wilde's later definition of hunting as 'the unspeakable in full pursuit of the uneatable'.

Drink may or may not have been Anne's secret vice: greed was certainly her public one. In this respect she took after her mother, James's first wife, Anne Hyde, who was renowned for her appetite. Anne and George did not go in for elaborate entertainment but dinner parties, still cooked by Patrick Lambe, were given in Sir Christopher Wren's elegant Orangery at Kensington Palace.

✣

PUPTON OF PIGEONS

This is a typical late seventeenth-century, early eighteenth-century dish. Pigeons had been popular with the rich for hundreds of years and most large houses kept a pigeon cote to ensure a constant supply. This recipe is from Patrick Lambe's book, *Royal Cookery, or the Complete Court Cook*, published in 1710.

100 g (4 oz) butter
2 pigeons
1 onion, sliced
25 g (1 oz) flour
1 teaspoon grated nutmeg
750 ml (1½ pints) game or chicken
    stock
2 cloves
salt and freshly ground black
    pepper
1 sweetbread, blanched and diced
    (see page 127)

100 g (4 oz) button mushrooms,
    diced
10 chestnuts, blanched and sliced
4 bacon rashers
juice of half a lemon
25 g (1 oz) butter
25 g (1 oz) fresh white
    breadcrumbs

TO SERVE:
juice of one large orange
fresh parsley

Melt the butter in a saucepan and brown the pigeons on all sides. Remove the pigeons and brown the onion in the same fat. Add the flour and nutmeg and cook for about a minute, scraping around the pan, until the flour is pale brown.

Add the stock and bring to the boil, stirring, until it begins to thicken. Place the pigeons in the stock, add the cloves and season.

Simmer the pigeons gently in the stock for about 50 minutes until tender. Remove the pigeons and discard the cloves and any pieces of onion.

Add the sweetbread, mushrooms and chestnuts to the stock and continue simmering until the stock is thick and creamy and reduced to about 375 ml (¾ pint). (About 15 minutes.)

While the pigeons are cooking make up the forcemeat as directed below. Line a well-buttered, deep, ovenproof dish with bacon rashers. Reserve enough of the forcemeat to make a 'crust' on the dish about 2.5 cm (1 in) thick. Mould the rest of the forcemeat round the bottom and sides of the dish.

Divide the cooked pigeons in half and lay them, breast down, on the forcemeat. Squeeze the lemon juice over the pigeons. Pour the reduced sauce around and over the pigeons. Do not overfill the dish. Reserve any extra sauce to serve separately.

Seal the dish securely with the remaining forcemeat. Dot with butter, sprinkle with breadcrumbs and bake at 180°C (350°F)/Gas 4 until cooked. (About 1½ hours.) Remove from the oven. Leave to cool for about 5 minutes, then unmould carefully on to a warmed serving dish. Squeeze the orange juice over the top, and garnish with parsley.

FOR THE FORCEMEAT:
325 g (¾ lb) fresh white breadcrumbs
450 ml (18 fl oz) milk
50 g (2 oz) bacon rashers, diced
450 g (1 lb) ground veal
75 g (3 oz) shredded suet
1 clove garlic, crushed
1 tablespoon fresh parsley, finely chopped
1 tablespoon of any available fresh herbs (except mint), finely chopped
½ teaspoon ground nutmeg
2 egg yolks, beaten
1 egg white, whipped stiff
salt and freshly ground black pepper

Soak the breadcrumbs in hot milk for about 30 minutes to allow them to swell up. Drain off the excess liquid.

Fry the bacon in a heavy frying pan until the fat runs. Add the veal and the suet and fry gently for about 10 minutes. Remove frying pan from heat and mix in the breadcrumbs, garlic, herbs and nutmeg. Beat in the egg yolks. Fold in the beaten egg white. Season well.

SERVES 6

GEORGE I

(1714–1727)

✣ ✣

GEORGE I was never popular with the English, and he in his turn did not like England much. He would far rather have returned to his native country, the Electorate of Hanover. It was firmly believed by the English that the governing of England was too great a task for the indolent and somewhat stupid sovereign. Certainly he never learned to speak English, and his indifference was so great that he left all matters of government to his ministers and so was indirectly responsible for the sort of government by Parliament that we have today.

When he came to England he left behind his wife, Sophie Dorothea. She had been divorced by him because of an affair, and from that time, when she was twenty-eight, until her death aged sixty-one, she was kept a prisoner in the castle of Ahlden. George's cruelty was so great that he never allowed her to see her children again, even though they managed to keep in touch spasmodically. The absence of their Queen was never explained to the English.

George cared only for what was German and that applied to his mistresses. He brought over to England with him two rather bizarre-looking ladies. One, who was tall and thin, was given the English title of Countess of Darlington, and nicknamed by the English 'The Maypole' . The other, who was short and fat, was given the title of Duchess of Kendal. The English called her 'The Elephant'. It was 'The Elephant', a woman considered something of an idiot, whom George preferred, and who had the greatest influence over him. He had a penchant for large women. Lord Chesterfield wrote of his amours 'No woman came amiss of him, if they were *very willing* and *very fat.*' It appeared that in spite of his unpleasant character and appearance there were quite a few ladies who *were* willing. These went to some lengths to gain the King's attentions. Lord Chesterfield goes on to say that in their efforts to appear the required weight they 'strain and swell themselves like the frog in the fable to rival the bulk and dignity of the ox. Some succeeded, others burst.'

Along with his fat German mistress George liked fattening German food. He brought German cooks over with him to replace the English ones, and food at court became distinctly heavy and frequently dull. Like many of his predecessors George liked to eat great quantities, and he was immensely corpulent. One filling German dish that he introduced to this country was the suet pudding and George was called the 'Pudding King' either because of the advent of the dish during his reign or maybe because he looked like one. A variation of the suet pudding, the apple dumpling, was the subject of a couplet in which the English mocked the stupidity of their fat, dull monarch.

> How? cried the staring monarch with a grin –
> How the Devil got the apple in?

But pudding was not always dull. English Christmas, or plum, pudding is one of the most delicious dishes in the world. A French man, Monsieur Mission, who came to England during George's reign wrote:

> Blessed be he that invented the pudding, for it is a Manna that hits the palates of all sorts of People. A manna better than that of the Wilderness, because the people are never weary of it. Ah, what an excellent thing is an English Pudding ! To come in Pudding Time, is as much as to say, to come in the most lucky Moment in the World.

✢

PLUM PUDDING

This is a traditional plum pudding like the ones served to George I. These quantities will make one large pudding or two small ones.

225 g (8 oz) prunes	*350 g (12 oz) shredded beef suet*
275 g (10 oz) sultanas	*225 g (8 oz) self-raising flour*
275 g (10 oz) currants	*½ level teaspoon salt*
225 g (8 oz) raisins	*1 level teaspoon ground nutmeg*
1 small lemon	*½ level teaspoon ground*
100 g (4 oz) dates	*cinnamon*
225 g (8 oz) mixed peel	*2 level teaspoons mixed spice*
50 g (2 oz) glacé cherries	*350 g (12 oz) soft, brown sugar*
225 g (8 oz) fresh brown	*4 eggs*
breadcrumbs	*100 ml (4 fl oz) brandy*

Soak the prunes overnight in cold water. Wash the sultanas, currants and raisins. Spread on a tray and leave to dry overnight. Grate the lemon rind and squeeze out the juice. Stone the prunes and chop roughly. Chop the dates roughly. Mix all the dried and glace fruits, breadcrumbs, suet, lemon juice and rind in a bowl.

Add the sifted flour, salt, spices and sugar. Mix thoroughly. Beat the eggs together in a jug and stir them gradually into the mixture in the bowl. Mix thoroughly.

Add the brandy a little at a time. The mixture should be of a stiff but dropping consistency. If it seems too stiff add a little milk.

Grease 2 x 1 litre (2 pint) pudding basins. Fill the basins with the pudding mixture to within about 5cm (2 in) of the rim. Wrap each basin in a pudding cloth or aluminium foil.

Place in separate large saucepans, so that the water comes three quarters of the way up the sides of the basins. Cover and boil for 6 hours, topping up with more boiling water from time to time.

Allow puddings to cool. Remove cloth and greaseproof paper and cover with fresh greaseproof paper and foil. Store in a cool dry place. Boil for a further 2–3 hours before serving.

To make a traditional round Christmas pudding, wring out a large square of strong cotton in boiling water and dredge it well with flour. Turn the pudding into the centre of the cloth. Draw the ends of the cloth together and tie securely with string. Leave a little leeway for the pudding to expand and round out.

Place the pudding, tied ends uppermost, in boiling water. Boil for 6 hours without letting the water go off the boil. You will need to check the water level very frequently.

Hang in a cool, dry place to store. Boil for a further 2–3 hours before serving.

The pudding is traditionally served with a piece of holly stuck in the top. Brandy is poured over it and set alight. This will be more successful if you pour a little of the spirit into the dish round the pudding and light this first.

Serve the pudding with a brandy-flavoured egg custard.

✣

GEORGE II

(1727–1760)

✤ ✤

THE COURT of George II was not a particularly exciting place but anything would have been preferable to things as they had been under George I. The English managed to show a little more enthusiasm for the new monarch than they had for the old. This may in part have been because George's reign coincided with an upswing in English prosperity and influence. The Indian Empire was founded; General Wolfe finally defeated the French in Canada; and the Young Pretender was defeated in the famous '45, killing off any hope of real opposition to the Hanoverians.

George's great virtue was his personal courage. He was in fact the last English King to lead his troops into battle, when he won the Battle of Dettingen, and throughout his reign he had to be restrained from a mad desire to rush off to war at the drop of a hat. Other than bravery, he did not have much to recommend him. In

121

the true Hanoverian tradition he had quarrelled almost irreconcil-
ably with his eldest son, Frederick. His temper was not improved
by a tendency to suffer from piles. His morals were rather lax, and
he never managed to behave with quite the dignity required of a
monarch. His wife, Caroline of Ansbach, a shrewd, intelligent and
charming lady, was the really popular member of the family. She
did much to improve the royal image in the country. It was an
image which needed some polishing, for after an initial pro-
English period George had become like his father, despising
everything English and longing for what was German. Lord
Hervey wrote:

> There was nothing English ever commended in his presence
> that he did not show, or pretend to show, was surpassed by
> something of the kind in Germany. No English or even French
> cook could dress a dinner; no English coachman could drive, or
> English jockey ride, nor were any English horses fit to be drove
> or fit to be ridden; no Englishman knew how to come into a
> room nor any English woman how to dress herself.

Clearly not an easy man to please.

Queen Caroline did manage to get round him all the same, and
in his own way he was devoted to her, even rather dominated by
her, though he had the inevitable quota of royal mistresses.
Unfortunately, she died early, after an operation for a stomach
complaint. Even on her deathbed she was concerned for the
King's interests and anxious to manipulate the future as far as possible. As he sobbed at her bedside she advised him to marry again
should she die. George, overcome by emotion, and wishing to
make it quite clear she was irreplaceable, managed to utter in broken tones, 'Never, I shall have mistresses instead.'

He seems to have been commendably true to his promise, and
had many mistresses. These were often introduced to him by
despairing ministers anxious to take his mind off the possibility of
a good war, and prevent him from doing anything rash. Two ladies

seem to have been his particular favourites, the Countess Doloraine, and Lady Yarmouth, a German. There was fierce rivalry between these two, which was resolved in the undignified fashion to be expected of anything concerned with George. It seems that during a game of cards one evening at Kensington Palace, one of George's daughters pulled a chair from under Countess Doloraine who landed on the floor. George's mirth at the sight was uncontrollable and the Countess was deeply humiliated. She rose to her feet and whisked George's chair from under him so that he in turn landed on the floor. Lord Hervey, who tells the story explains 'But alas! the Monarch, like Louis XIV, is mortal in the part that touched the ground.' His sense of humour vanishing immediately, George ordered the poor, disgraced Countess out, and Lady Yarmouth was sole favourite from then on.

George's terrible rages, aggravated by the discomfort caused by his piles, were a fairly frequent occurrence at court. On one occasion he came rushing in on a family gathering, berated his children for no apparent reason, and stormed at his wife, who was getting old and not a little fat, for constantly 'stuffing herself with chocolate'. The poor woman cannot have had much other consolation, living with such a man.

Chocolate, and two other non-alcoholic drinks, tea and coffee, had caused something of a revolution in English drinking habits since they had first been introduced into the country in the middle of the previous century. The first public coffee house in Britain was opened in 1650 in Oxford. In 1657 a chocolate shop was opened in Bishopsgate, London, and in 1658 tea was first served, strangely enough, in a coffee shop. In the eighteenth century more and more rich people were drinking coffee, tea and chocolate at home. It is not surprising that Queen Caroline put on weight, for all three drinks were taken with large amounts of sugar. By the end of the eighteenth century the English consumption of sugar was fifteen times what it had been at the beginning. Controversies raged about the merits and the demerits of these three drinks. Not only did they clearly make you fat, they were considered at various times to be bad for health and morals. The ruling politicians saw danger in the free flow of speculation and gossip that went on in the atmosphere of the coffee shops. Do-gooders saw a danger to the poor who were spending money on tea (which was iniquitously expensive) when they should have been spending it on good food and shoes for their children. One undoubted benefit of tea at least was the money it made for Britain, whose East India company had an almost total monopoly in the product.

One other culinary happening must be mentioned in connection with the reign of George II, and that is the introduction, in fact the invention, of English mustard as we know it today. Tewkesbury mustard had been famous in the sixteenth and seventeenth centuries: Shakespeare mentions someone whose 'wit is as thicke as Tewkesburie mustard'. Then, in 1720 a Mrs Clements of Durham discovered how to mill mustard seed. The resulting bright yellow mustard paste rapidly became popular and was a great favourite with George II and his family.

✣

HOT CHOCOLATE

Chocolate was rarely eaten in block form at this time, but was usually made into a warming hot drink. It must have been more than a little welcome to the occupants of the royal residences, which were famous for their draughts. Blocks of chocolate would be bought from the specialist chocolate shops and the prepared drink was served in delicate porcelain basins held in silver holders, rather like present-day Russian tea cups. Special sets were sold for making and serving chocolate. As well as a pot and drinking cups these included little silver graters for grating the blocks of chocolate. Hot chocolate could be served at any time, but became very popular as a breakfast drink. This is no longer an English breakfast drink, but in Spain the custom has continued and real hot chocolate, made in a similar traditional manner, is served for breakfast to this day.

100 g (4 oz) plain chocolate
375 ml (¾ pint) water
375 ml (¾ pint) milk

2 eggs, beaten
12 g (½ oz) castor sugar

Break or grate the chocolate into the milk and water. Bring slowly to the boil in a saucepan, stirring constantly with a wire whisk. Simmer gently for about 15 minutes, still stirring. Remove from heat and allow to cool.

Whisk in the beaten eggs and sugar. Return to the heat and bring just to the boil, stirring constantly with the wire whisk to prevent the eggs from curdling.

Remove pan from the heat. Whisk mixture hard to create a good froth. Pour into warmed cups, making sure each cup has a good topping of froth.

SERVES 4–6

✤

TEA

Tea at this time was so expensive that it was kept in locked containers away from thieving hands. It was generally China tea, drunk without milk. This is one of many recipes where the tea is made into something rather more nourishing than the brew we are familiar with today. The inclusion of wine may have been one of the reasons why some people objected to it.

250 ml (½ pint) freshly made
  China tea
2 egg yolks, beaten

125 ml (¼ pint) dry white wine
¼ teaspoon grated nutmeg
sugar

Pour the tea into a heavy saucepan with the egg yolks, wine and nutmeg. Bring just to the point of boiling, stirring continuously. Serve with sugar to taste.

SERVES 2–3

✤

GEORGE III

(1760–1820)

✣ ✣

TWO FACTS stand out in relation to George III. He was the King who lost England the American colonies and he was the King who went completely mad in his old age. These things apart, George's time on the throne may be considered something of a success. He endeared himself to the English by showing a preference for England over Germany, by a mild eccentricity, and by the exemplary private life he led with his Queen, Charlotte, and their sixteen children.

The emphasis on domesticity and domestic economy which permeated George's entire life may in part have been a deliberate reaction against the exploits of the rest of his family. Certainly during his final years, when he suffered long periods of apparent insanity, there seem to be indications that it was the strain of a life-time's repression that was taking its toll. He pursued one middle-aged matron in particular, making lewd suggestions, and insisting she was his real wife. To Charlotte herself he made equally lewd suggestions, much to the embarrassment of the

126

accompanying ladies-in-waiting, who shouldn't have known what he was talking about anyway. Charlotte, too, seems to have suffered from what was, on the surface, a life of unruffled domestic harmony. George insisted that his household go to bed at ten o'clock, just when the rest of the fashionable world was preparing to enjoy itself. Shortly after her marriage Charlotte who was a lively young girl, insisted that nothing would make her go to bed with the chickens. Her resistance was eventually worn down, by boredom, endless child-bearing and what seems to have been a deliberate policy to deprive her of anyone adult to speak to except the King. She seems to have become a very repressed lady, whose children disliked and mistrusted her. Even when the children were little, George seemed unable to let her have any real influence on their upbringing, preferring to supervise every detail himself. He was a devoted father but many of his theories were rather bizarre. The children were allowed only two meals a day, the last being at two o'clock in the afternoon. It is not surprising that his sons were renowned as adults for their appalling over-indulgence. They probably had a lurking fear that if they did not eat everything at once it might be taken away. George's unrelenting insistence on organizing everyone the way it suited him affected his daughters even when they grew up. Unlike their brothers they had no chance of freedom and a separate household, unless they married. George did not like the idea of their marrying and leaving home, so they remained trapped, writing letters to their envied brothers inscribed 'from the nunnery'.

George was nicknamed 'Farmer George' because of his preference for the simple rustic life which he tried to recreate at his palace at Kew. He did not regard this title as offensive, but as a great compliment. Farming was his hobby, and he was particularly interested in it for he hoped it might be a hobby that paid its own way. Economy certainly seems to have been his watchword, and his economies were fairly drastic and not in keeping with his exalted position. One of his main economies was to cut out food and drink when entertaining. At a party for the birth of his eldest son, which came to be known scornfully as the 'gingerbread affair', there were few guests, no food, and everyone was packed off home before they quite knew why they had come. He gave a fête in the grounds of Windsor Castle for the boys from nearby Eton School, where they were deeply disappointed by a long recital of religious music and a complete absence of any food or drink. Even his coronation feast was held with a strict eye to economy. When inflation and poor harvests inevitably forced costs up, George still refused to accept defeat but insisted on accusing his local Windsor greengrocers, Mr and Mrs Miller, of overcharging. Finally he refused to buy from them. The loss of royal patronage is thought to have sent poor Mr Miller to a suicide's grave. Hearty guests of the Royal Family, returning from many hours of hard hunting, were appalled to find that when George asked them if they would like a drink he was referring to barley water. His meanness was well known: satires of the time portray the domesticated King and Queen making their own butter in the royal dairies and preparing their own food.

Part of the trouble seems to have been that George himself was very abstemious, and being totally inflexible he was unable to see anything from anyone else's point of view. Poor Charlotte may have felt it was advisable to accept the role so rigidly laid down for her, and spend her evenings at home accompanying her husband on the harpsichord, while he played his flute. She may have been prepared to concede on the upbringing of her children, she may even have coped with the lack of any company, but it is rather sad to think of her sending to Germany for smoked sausage in order to make the parsimonious household a little more tolerable. George was very aware of the family tendency to run to fat. His uncle, the Duke of Cumberland, was so obese that when he fell over while dancing, very appropriately, at a party given by Lord Sandwich, 'He lay like a tortoise on its shell, his face could not reach the ground.' With this in mind George treated his eating habits like everything else. He set himself almost impossible standards and expected other people to stick to them with him. When congratulated on only ever eating one slice of toast for breakfast in an age when people ate themselves silly he replied, ''Tis no virtue. I only prefer eating plain and little to growing diseased and infirm.' He drank no more than four glasses of wine at dinner, and his guests were expected to do the same.

Just as he expected people to enjoy his parties, without food or drink, simply for the pleasure of being invited, he expected artists and actors to give their services in exchange for nothing but the honour of his patronage. The actress Mrs Siddons was made preceptress in English to his daughters and taught them each week for no reward whatsoever. The portrait painter Thomas Lawrence also gave his services free.

George seems to have spared himself nothing in achieving the standards he seems at some point to have decided on for himself. He was the only person who could stand the cold and draughts of the royal palaces. So of course nothing was done for the more susceptible souls living there. The entire household would start the winter attending morning service daily in the unheated stone chapel at Windsor, and by the time spring was beginning the only member to have survived without succumbing to a foul cold was George himself. The absence of any of those who should have been there was not looked upon kindly, for George was a stickler for etiquette and all the formality of court procedure. Poor shortsighted Fanny Burney, the novelist who was for some time Assistant Keeper of the Queen's Wardrobe, was not allowed to wear the spectacles she so badly needed because it just was not done, and suffered from terrible headaches in consequence.

George did occasionally let his hair down. He was very fond of the theatre, especially slapstick and pantomime. Even so he was careful to censor Charlotte's viewing, for whenever anything happened on stage of which he disapproved he would say to her in his funny manner, 'Don't look ! It's too much.'

His long illness was a traumatic affair for himself and his family. The unhappy George was forced to spend long periods in a straitjacket, to eat disgusting 'medicines' and to do as he was told. During this period his son, Prince George, reigned as Regent, and the old King was virtually forgotten.

✣

FLOATING ISLANDS

At the end of the eighteenth century there seems to have been a glut of pudding recipes. It was something like the medieval passion for food which looked as good or better than it tasted that prompted this English delight in elaborate puddings. *Floating Islands* fulfilled all the requirements, being curious and impressive to look at and sufficiently sweet and self-indulgent to be enjoyed. There are several versions of this pudding. This recipe is typical of the time when George and Charlotte would have eaten it.

250 ml (½ pint) double cream
75 ml (3 fl oz) sweet white wine
12 g (½ oz) castor sugar
grated rind of half a lemon
whites of two eggs

1 heaped tablespoon redcurrant
  jelly

TO DECORATE:
langue de chat biscuits
crystallized flowers or fruit

Beat the cream with the wine, sugar and lemon rind until it is thickened but not stiff. Spread the cream in a wide shallow dish to form the 'sea'. Beat the egg whites with the jelly until they are stiff enough to form peaks. Spoon the flavoured egg white onto the cream to form an 'island'. Peak the egg whites with a fork. Place crystallized flowers or fruit on the egg white. Make a decorative border with the *langue de chat* biscuits. Additional decoration, for example with fresh flowers, makes the dish even more attractive.

SERVES 4–6

✣

GEORGE IV

(1820–1830)

✣ ✣

GEORGE WAS his parents' adored elder son who eventually caused a great deal of misery by his complete rejection of their cosy lifestyle for a wanton and flippant way of life. He was not stupid, far from it, nor was he deliberately cruel. Although he could be vindictive to his fashionable acquaintances he was horrified by any sort of cruelty to animals and he did his best to prevent the execution of several criminals, for he found the whole idea of capital punishment abhorrent. It may have been that like Edward VII nearly one hundred years later he was stifled by having nothing to do except wait until the reigning monarch died; a process which in both their cases entailed a very long wait indeed. By the time he reached the throne he was despised by the people and his short reign did nothing to redress the balance.

As a young man George had been a rather pretty dandy, adored by the ladies and revelling in his position as a leader of fashion. Unfortunately fashion and the fashionable way of life seemed to mean everything to him. He loathed snuff but it was fashionable to take it. He would therefore go through all the ritual of elegant posturing involved in opening a costly snuff box. but to the amusement of those who watched him he always managed to allow the powder to escape between his finger and thumb before it actually got to his nose. Clothes were a passion with him: he could not bear to throw any of them away and when he died all the coats he had owned over the last fifty years were found in his wardrobes. He was encouraged in his extravagant tastes by the famous dandy 'Beau' Brummell, until the pair of them quarrelled and Brummell was cast into the cold exile of social unacceptability.

George's real problem was a total lack of will-power and of any ability to say no. It meant that he spent all his money on extravagant entertainment that neither he nor his parsimonious father could afford. One of his best-known pieces of self-indulgence is the Royal Pavilion at Brighton. This building, rather incongruous in what was then a simple fishing village, is decorated lavishly in the Chinese style so fashionable at the time. In building it and furnishing it in the epitome of fashion George went into debt from which he never recovered. His taste for extravagant projects is seen also in the Nash terraces around Regent's Park and in the architecture of Regent Street, which leads towards it. This uncompleted project, uncompleted because of lack of funds, was intended to turn the North London park into a private park for the prince and his cronies. He constantly needed the distraction of new projects on a small scale as well as this large scale. A contemporary summed up the immaturity of his approach to life by saying that he 'grew peevish if there was not a perpetual rattle for him'.

His immaturity was apparent in his attitude to women and in his attitude to his marriage in particular. Although prevented from doing so by the Royal Marriage Act, which laid down specific requirements for the spouse of any member of the Royal Family, George married a young, Catholic commoner, a widow called Mrs Fitzherbert. The marriage was secret and was not strictly valid because of George's situation, but it satisfied Mrs Fitzherbert, who regarded herself as the prince's real wife. She was known to the wags of the day as 'The Lass of Richmond Hill'. George remained surprisingly faithful to her by his standards for many years. She was older than he was and it was a feature that all his mistresses seemed to have in common. In later life he made himself ludicrous with a succession of ageing, overweight ladies who seem to have fulfilled a mother role more than anything else. It did nothing for George's reputation in the country, for people resented his over-eating, his overdrinking, his foppishness and his fat mistresses being paraded in front of them, at a time when Britain was engaged in a crucial war with Napoleon, and even facing the threat of a French invasion.

In spite of his 'marriage' to Mrs Fitzherbert, the prince was required to marry for political reasons. The lady chosen for the honour was his cousin, Caroline of Brunswick, who was short, slightly deformed and not a little tainted with the family mania. When George was first introduced to her he cried out for brandy! Among her many unattractive features was the fact that she was rather smelly. George hated her on sight and never stopped hating her. He would rather, he said, have toads and vipers crawling all over his victuals than sit down at the same table with her. Their marriage day was a farce: George's current mistress, Lady Jersey, helped dress the unwitting bride in a most unbecoming outfit and then sprinkled Epsom salts on her food at the wedding supper. George left Caroline for good shortly after the birth of their only child, Princess Charlotte, and Mrs Fitzherbert gave a public party to celebrate his return to the fold. Caroline continued to get dottier and dottier, and took up with a string of gigolo-like lovers, which prompted George to try to divorce her. He was forced to give up the attempt but took his revenge for the defeat by refusing to let her attend his coronation. The Great British Public, appalled at this behaviour, took Caroline's cause to heart and George's popularity took another plunge.

One of George's pleasanter characteristics was the fact that he was an excellent and generous host. He was also a gourmet as well as a glutton. When the Royal Pavilion had been built he brought over to this country the famous French chef Carême. It was the second time that French cookery was going through a phase when it was considered to be pre-eminent (the first time was the seventeenth century), and Carême was one of the first and greatest among the exponents of what we now think of as haute cuisine. He was the youngest of twenty-five children and had begun his training very, very young by working in a pastry shop for his food, because his parents could not afford to keep him. He became a specialist in the elaborate *pièces montées* which were the equivalent of the medieval *soteltes* – fantastic creations to decorate the table. He made many of these for the banquets held by Napoleon and had also worked for a while for Tsar Alexander of Russia.

Carême was utterly and completely dedicated to cooking and to food When he was a Master Pastry Cook, which might have been considered good enough by most people, he would study at night after a long and exhausting day in the kitchens, so that eventually he was a master of every branch of the culinary art. The prince considered himself extremely fortunate to entice him over to England, but Carême stayed for only two years in spite of the incredible offers to make him stay longer. He found the prince, although kind enough, was too ignorant on the subject of food, and the English staff he was expected to work with were even more so. It may partly have been because Carême never mastered English, but he was undeniably homesick for France and returned there as soon as he could, vowing never to leave again. He had been impressed by the quality of the raw materials, the meat and vegetables, which he had to work with in England, but he was horrified by the standard of cooking. Admittedly his standards were unbelievably exacting, for his dedication was almost religious. The heat and fumes of the kitchens of the time, which were equipped with coal- and wood-burning stoves and ovens, were appalling, especially in a kitchen where food was prepared every day for hundreds of people. Carême wrote 'Le charbon nous tue, mais qu'importe? Moins de jours, plus de gloire!' He was a stickler for hygiene, unlike most of his English counterparts, and the new kitchens at Brighton must have been a joy to him, for they were the ultimate in efficiency. For perhaps the first time ever, they showed that kitchens could be planned for ease of work and not just set up in a haphazard fashion.

George's fondness for food soon manifested itself in his ever-increasing corpulence. It did not take long for the attractive, if rather feckless, young dandy to become an obese and ludicrous middle-aged man. As he became more immobile he took to spending long hours sitting down drinking cherry brandy and eating large plates of roast beef. He did once try to go on a diet to impress his new mistress, Lady Conyngham, who was no slender reed herself, but the rot had set in too far. His idle way of life took its toll on his appearance and his character, and when he died few people cared. Some even celebrated.

✥

SALMIS OF QUAILS WITH MADEIRA WINE
The influence of Carême, and of French cooking generally, on English cuisine, has lasted to this day. One of the most interesting developments was the use of entrées as main courses. The entrées used to be dishes which filled in the gaps between the main dishes of the different courses – the roast meats and the beloved English pies. While Carême reigned supreme in the royal kitchens this remained their main function, but they were developed and elaborated to such an extent that today in most restaurants they are offered as the main course. This did not happen immediately, because Carême was one of the old school who believed in presenting a whole course, main dishes, entremets (now usually just

served as desserts) and entrées, on the table at one time. He was concerned with the overall look of the thing. The table as he set it was indeed an amazing sight, laden with food and dominated by the incredible centre pieces which he concocted. The disadvantage was that the food was inevitably cold by the time it was eaten. A second disadvantage from the guest's point of view was that in spite of an apparent choice, he was pretty well stuck with whatever was nearest to him. After this, cooks who were concerned that their food should be appreciated hot from the kitchens gradually won the day. The number of dishes offered was reduced and entrées became almost invariably a course in their own right, which makes their name rather confusing today.

Salmis of Quails is one of the most typical entrées of the period and was served to the Prince Regent at Brighton many times. Real stock, and *Espagnole Sauce* made with real stock, should be used or the dish will be nothing like as delicious as when the Prince Regent ate it.

8 prepared quails	*2 shallots, thinly sliced*
50 g (2 oz) butter for basting	*250 ml (½ pint) Madeira wine*
125 ml (¼ pint) freshly made game or chicken stock	*250 ml (½ pint) Espagnole Sauce (see page 141)*
thinly grated rind of half an orange	*croûtons*
	1 orange, peeled and sectioned

Make the *Espagnole Sauce* one or two days in advance.

Lightly roast the quails in a hot oven 220°C (425°F)/Gas 7 for about 15–20 minutes. Baste them very frequently with the butter.

Remove the skin from the cooked quails and cut off the leg and wing joints and the breasts as neatly as possible. Keep them warm.

Break up the quail carcases and put them in a pan with the stock, orange rind, shallots and half the wine. Simmer gently for 30 minutes, stirring occasionally. Strain this stock through a sieve into the *Espagnole Sauce*. Press the bones well to extract all the flavour. Add the remaining wine.

Reheat the meat gently in the sauce for about 10 minutes. Remove the meat from the sauce and arrange on a hot serving dish. Continue boiling the sauce for a few minutes until it is a fairly syrupy consistency. Meanwhile fry the croûtons.

Pour the sauce over the quail joints. Garnish with orange sections and croûtons. Serve immediately.

SERVES 4

LE SAUTÉ DE RIS DE VEAU À LA PROVENÇALE

This is another entrée served by the famous French chef Carême to the Prince Regent at the newly-built Royal Pavilion at Brighton.

450 g (1 lb) calf's sweetbreads,   *juice of half a lemon*
(Carême would have used the   *2 eggs, beaten*
more delicate 'heart'   *dried breadcrumbs*
sweetbreads)   *butter and olive oil for frying*

Soak the sweetbreads for 3–4 hours in cold water. Drain. Blanch the sweetbreads by placing them in a saucepan, covering them with cold water and the juice of half a lemon, bringing the water slowly to the boil and simmering for 5 minutes. Drain. Leave in a bowl of cold water for about 30 minutes until cool and firm. Discard any tough or stringy tissue.

When the sauce is made and you are ready to serve the sweetbreads remove them from the water and dry them thoroughly between pieces of kitchen paper. Cut them into bite-sized pieces. Dip the pieces in the beaten egg and breadcrumbs. Sauté in a little butter and olive oil until a light golden brown.

Pile the sweetbreads in the centre of a heated dish and serve with the sauce poured round.

FOR THE SAUCE:
50 g (2 oz) unsalted butter
4 shallots, finely chopped
2 cloves garlic, skinned and
   crushed
100 g (4 oz) white, button
   mushrooms, quartered
250 ml (½ pint) dry white wine

900 g (2 lb) fresh tomatoes,
   skinned, deseeded and chopped
1 tablespoon fresh parsley, finely
   chopped
3 teaspoons tomato purée
4 teaspoons sugar
2 bay leaves
salt and freshly ground black
   pepper

Melt the butter and fry the shallots and garlic very gently until soft but not brown. Push to one side of the pan and add the mushrooms. Fry gently for 2 minutes. Remove pan from the heat and add the remaining ingredients. Return to the heat and simmer gently for about 20 minutes until the sauce reduces and thickens. Season to taste.

SERVES 3–4

✤

Either of these entrées may be served with boiled rice. Among the vegetables mentioned on the same menu are potatoes with *Hollandaise Sauce, Mushrooms à la Provençale* and a purée of haricot beans. As a first course serve fish soup. As a dessert (or entremet) choose chocolate or apricot soufflé.

✤

ᙡILLIAM IV

(1830–1837)

✤ ✤

ᏀEORGE'S BROTHER had never expected to come to the throne himself and had pursued a career as a sailor. Inevitably he became known as 'The Sailor King'. The bluntness and candour associated with a sailor were an integral part of his character and the people loved him for it, especially after the affected excesses of George IV. He was so popular that he never had any fear of walking through the streets unaccompanied.

There are many stories of his unaffected, one must really say vulgar, manners and mannerisms, that were sometimes endearing, but sometimes a little hard to take. When the news of his accession was brought to him by messengers who had rushed through the night to reach him at six o'clock in the morning, he announced that he was returning immediately to bed as it had always been his ambition to sleep with a Queen. While King he attended a special dinner held for the diplomatic corps attached to the British court. Afterwards he was required to give a speech in French, which was the language of diplomacy. Unfortunately he had drunk rather too much and got rather carried away, ending up with a toast to 'Les yeux qui tuent, les fesses qui remuent, et le cul qui danse, honi soit qui mal y pense.' Asked what he thought of the speech, the French Ambassador could only reply 'C'est bien remarquable.' Other naval habits were less amusing: wiping his nose with the back of his finger and spitting out of his carriage window.

William's wife, Queen Adelaide, was not a sparkling personality and the court became rather a dull place compared with the immediate past. William, who was sixty-five when he came to the throne, was always amiable but he did tend to snooze gently through parties. Yet there had been a time when he had been far from dull company. In his youth he had loved dancing and pretty women. He had a long-lasting liaison with a famous actress of the time, Mrs Jordan, who bore him numerous children and even helped him eke out the meagre allowance he got from his father with the money she earned from acting. When William realized, after the death of George IV's daughter, that he would probably be the next King he pensioned off Mrs Jordan and married the dull but highly respectable Adelaide. Mrs Jordan, who had been a faithful and loyal companion for so long, seems literally to have died of a broken heart.

Before their relationship came to such a sad end the house which William kept with Mrs Jordan was a lively and hospitable place famous for its extravagant parties. They never had any money but that did not seem to prevent them from spending it. Balls and dinners were given by William on board his ship the *Andromeda*. Mrs Jordan would act as hostess on these occasions and as dawn broke a breakfast of cold meats was served, in which cold turkey, one of William's favourites, usually featured. William loved to drink and even more he loved to get people drunk. If he saw anyone abstaining or drinking modestly he would force them to drink endless loyal toasts, something it was very difficult to refuse to do in the presence of the King's son, until they eventually collapsed. On one occasion he was entertaining his niece Charlotte and her husband, Prince Leopold of Saxe-Coburg, to dinner and the unfortunate Leopold was seen to be drinking water. William yelled at him in his hearty sailor's voice, 'What's that you're drinking, sir? Water, sir! God damn it! Why don't you drink wine? I never allow anybody to drink water.'

As King he continued to entertain on a lavish scale. On average two thousand people a week ate at his expense. The Duke of Buckingham remarked that on these occasions 'a nautical freedom prevailed which often gave a peculiar heartiness to the conversation, though strict etiquette was not unfrequently entirely lost sight of.' On his birthday in 1830 he gave a banquet at Windsor for all the poor people. There were places for three thousand, and boiled and roast beef, roast veal, hams and plum pudding were served. In 1834 thirty-six thousand bottles of wine were drunk at just one of the royal palaces.

In spite of his generosity William made economies on the extravagances of his brother George. The number of royal yachts was reduced from five to two. Fourteen thousand pounds a year was saved by dismissing George's German band and replacing it with a British substitute. Unfortunately economies included dismissing all the French cooks and there was a distinct decline in the standard of cooking. Lord Dudley, among others, noticed the decline. 'What a change to be sure – cold pâtés and hot champagne.' Yet by the time he died William had brought about another, more important change and that was a completely new and informal style of monarchy that has never really been reversed.

✧

LAMB CUTLETS WITH ESPAGNOLE SAUCE

Almost every day William ate a simple lunch of lamb cutlets accompanied by a few glasses of sherry. In doing so he was following the new style of somewhat simpler food, even from the royal kitchens, and the use of entrées as main dishes. *Espagnole Sauce* is so called because Spanish ham was originally used to make it, instead of bacon.

FOR THE STOCK:
900 g (2 lb) shin of beef with bone
butter or fat for frying
2 litres (4 pints) water
2 carrots, sliced

2 onions, sliced
1 bouquet garni
2 bay leaves
½ tablespoon black peppercorns
salt

Remove the meat from the bones and cube it, removing all the skin and fat. Brown the meat in the fat or butter. Transfer to a large saucepan, using a slotted spoon so that as much fat as possible is left behind. Add the bones, and the remaining ingredients to the saucepan. Bring to the boil and simmer gently for about 4 hours, skimming off the scum from time to time. Strain and leave to cool. When the stock is cold remove every trace of fat. This will make about 1 litre (2 pints) of strong stock.

FOR THE ESPAGNOLE SAUCE:
50 g (2 oz) butter
50 g (2 oz) bacon, diced
1 carrot, sliced
1 onion, sliced
1 bouquet garni
1 bay leaf
1 clove

4 peppercorns
35 g (1½ oz) cornflour
1 litre (2 pints) strong brown
   stock (see above)
75 ml (3 fl oz) dry sherry
3 tablespoons tomato purée
salt and pepper

Melt the butter in a heavy saucepan. Add the chopped bacon and vegetables and fry gently until golden. Add the herbs, clove and peppercorns. Stir into the butter and allow to sweat gently for 5 minutes. Add the cornflour and brown gently, adding a little more butter if necessary.

Remove the pan from the heat and add stock, sherry and tomato purée. Return to the heat, bring to the boil and simmer gently for 1½ hours. Strain the sauce and leave to cool. Skim off any fat, reheat and season before serving.

8 lamb cutlets
2 beaten eggs

dried breadcrumbs
8 small paper frills to serve

Scrape the last 1.5 cm (¾ in) of each cutlet bone bare of meat. Beat the cutlets a little to flatten them, so they are more or less a uniform shape. Dip the cutlets into the beaten egg and breadcrumbs, pressing the crumbs firmly on to the meat with a knife. Repeat if necessary to give a good coating. Grill under a very hot, preheated grill for about 2–3 minutes on either side. Place a paper frill on the end of each cutlet. Arrange on a heated flat dish surrounded by piped mashed potato. Serve with Espagnole Sauce and peas.

If you like your cutlets very well cooked omit the egg and breadcrumbs, which will char if overcooked. Brush the cutlets with melted butter instead.

SERVES 4

✣

Begin the meal with consommé or turtle soup. As a dessert serve the following lemon-flavoured cream, which was a great favourite with William.

✣

LEMON CREAM

2 small lemons or 65 ml (2½ fl oz)　　*1 teaspoon orange flower water*
*　lemon juice*　　　　　　　　　　*3 egg whites*
75 g (3 oz) castor sugar

Squeeze the juice from the lemons into a saucepan and mix it with the sugar, orange flower water and five teaspoons of cold water. Heat the mixture for a minute or so until the sugar has melted. Remove from the heat and allow to cool.

Beat the egg whites until stiff and stir them into the lemon mixture. Cook over a low heat, stirring constantly, until the mixture thickens.

Serve hot or cold.

SERVES 4

✣

VICTORIA

(1837–1901)

✦ ✦

QUEEN VICTORIA, who came to the throne at eighteen, reigned longer than any other monarch in English history. Right from the start her diet was a matter of comment, for the infant Victoria was breast-fed by her mother, an unusual occurrence in the Best Society of the day. Despite this, and despite the theories of modern nutritionists, she grew up to be an adult with a persistent and worsening weight problem. It was a problem exacerbated by the undeniable fact that Victoria liked her food.

As a young woman in the process of getting and keeping her man, Albert, with whom she was besotted, Victoria fought a constant battle against being overweight. Resolutions are recorded almost daily in her diary to 'eat only half a biscuit for luncheon', or 'to have no luncheon at all but a good breakfast'. She complained bitterly because – being under five feet tall – every extra pound, which might go unnoticed on a larger frame, was shown to devastating effect. Lord Melbourne's attempts to stop her dieting by assuring her that the best figure for a woman was 'fine and full with a full bust' did nothing to allay her anxieties. She tried to be seen as often as possible on horseback, knowing that being so far off the ground made her look more impressive than she was otherwise.

While Albert was alive, Victoria's taste in food and every other form of entertainment was dominated by his preferences, and what was good enough for Albert was considered more than good enough for the whole court. While Albert may not have been quite the caricature of a repressed Puritan that history has chosen to remember, he undoubtedly laid heavy emphasis on the simple and solid virtues. That went for food as well. Albert's stomach tended to be a little delicate, probably due to recurrent food poisoning from the royal kitchens rather than the fragile constitution for which Victoria gave him such credit. When they ate privately the couple had mainly plain food – boiled chicken, roast beef, haggis and Brown Windsor soup. It can hardly have been worth any chef's while to risk anything more exciting since Victoria was not above pulling faces at any dish she did not like.

It was state entertaining that gave the royal chefs the opportunity for more elaborate dishes. It would have been a great shame if they had been always restricted by Victoria's and Albert's preferences, for among the distinguished chefs who at some time or another worked for Victoria were Soyer, Ranieri, Francatelli and Menager. Soyer was a particularly interesting person. He was for a long time chef at the Reform Club and invented the flambé trolley. However his interests went beyond rich cooking for rich people. He tried to work out recipes which would enable the poor to nourish themselves adequately on a low income and even took out field kitchens to feed the soldiers fighting in the Crimean War. His motto was 'Cleanliness is the Soul of the kitchen.'

Victoria's sweet tooth meant that sweets and puddings were always plentiful on the royal table. She particularly liked cranberry tart with lots of cream, and shared Elizabeth I's love of anything made with cherries. The steamed and suet puddings brought to

England with the Hanoverians were revived in popularity by the arrival of the German Prince Albert. One steamed pudding is actually called Albert Pudding, but it seems more likely that these nourishing and warming puddings were eaten by Victoria's subjects rather than her family.

Like the food, the court entertainment was noted for its simplicity and, if truth be told, tedium. In the brief period between her accession and her marriage to Albert, Victoria's court and Victoria herself had enjoyed a reputation for light-heartedness and gaiety which is almost totally forgotten. Victoria used to stay up dancing until three in the morning and lie late in bed. Albert took it upon himself to wean his wife from such trivia and succeeded to the extent that a few years later the diarist Charles Greville wrote that the 'Great Difficulty in Royal Society' was getting through the tedious evenings.

But for Victoria life could never be dull with Albert by her side. She threw herself with enthusiasm into the simple, healthy, country way of life he preferred and to which they came nearest in their Scottish home at Balmoral. The couple became the epitome of domestic harmony. Victoria even bought Albert a silver lunch box to keep his sandwiches in when he was out hunting all day. In the morning Albert was allowed to read his *Times* (ironed of course) in silence, undisturbed by the chatter of wife and children. Christmas was celebrated in the German way with a Christmas tree hung with home-made sweets and toys. Christmas food was traditional roast goose and turkey, boar's head, plum pudding, mince pies, and champagne.

When Albert's death brought the lovely family way of life to an end, Victoria withdrew from public life almost completely. She found wining and dining foreign guests a particular strain without Albert at her side and was appalled at having to cope with the strange tastes of men like the King of Siam and the Shah of Persia. The Shah in particular caused Her Majesty a few tremors, for strange reports had come from the British Ambassador in Berlin where the Shah had already paid a visit. The Shah, it was said, had to have his food on a carpet and was quite likely to take a piece of well-chewed food out of his mouth, inspect it, and throw it under the table if it did not meet with his approval. In the event, the poor man turned out to be perfectly pleasant and civilized, but Victoria saw him depart with great relief.

As Albert's influence faded a little, Victoria branched out in one or two directions she would not have dreamed of before. Inside the house she forbade smoking and even had *No Smoking* notices put up in all the rooms but on picnics she would often smoke a cigarette herself to keep the insects away. Her faithful Scottish servant, John Brown, introduced her to whisky. Since anything from Scotland was all right with Victoria she took to the drink immediately even topping up her wine with it. The last thing she drank before she died was a glass of whisky.

Many years of overwork eventually ruined Victoria's digestion. In an attempt to improve the situation the Queen's Physician recommended a diet of chicken and Benger's Invalid Food. Unhappily the Queen was so delighted with the Benger's that she took to eating it in addition to her usual meals of roast beef and ice cream. Marie Mallet, one of her ladies-in-waiting, felt that the eighty-two-year-old Queen could hardly expect to avoid indigestion when she 'devours a huge chocolate ice, followed by a couple of apricots, washed down with iced water.' However Queen Victoria avoided the fate of several of her intemperate ancestors and died, not of indigestion, but simply because she had reached a good old age.

✣

TURBOT AU GRATIN

Although Victoria was not overfond of rich food, except curries, a lot of very rich dishes indeed were served at her table. Her first chef, Francatelli, quickly grew bored working for the Queen and left, but in the short time he was royal chef he concocted innumerable elaborate meals. *Turbot au Gratin* is one of the dishes he served and although it is rich it is simple enough to make in an ordinary kitchen not equipped with enormous ovens, gallons of different varieties of stock and bevies of hardworking servants. Halibut can be used as an alternative for this dish if turbot is not available.

FOR THE COURT BOUILLON:
1 litre (2 pints) water
250 ml (½ pint) white wine
1 onion, sliced
1 carrot, sliced

1 bay leaf
1 tablespoon fresh parsley
1 teaspoon black peppercorns
½ teaspoon salt

Place all the ingredients in a sauce-pan, bring to the boil and simmer for 30 minutes. Strain.

FOR THE CREAM SAUCE:
25 g (1 oz) butter
25 g (1 oz) cornflour
150 ml (6 fl oz) milk
250 ml (½ pint) cooking liquor
  from the fish (see below)
1 egg yolk

1½ tablespoons grated Parmesan
  cheese
125 ml (¼ pint) double cream
squeeze of lemon juice
salt and freshly ground black
  pepper
small pinch nutmeg

Melt the butter and stir in the cornflour to make a smooth white roux. Keeping the pan over a gentle heat gradually stir in the milk and fish liquor to make a smooth sauce. Beat in the egg yolk, cheese and cream. Season lightly to taste with the lemon juice, salt, pepper and nutmeg.

1 piece of turbot, about 1.2 kg
  (2½ lb)
1 lemon
25 g (1 oz) unsalted butter

75 g (3 oz) fresh white
  breadcrumbs
75 g (3 oz) grated Parmesan
  cheese

Rub the white sides of the fish with a cut lemon. Place the fish in a large pan, cover with the court bouillon and poach gently until cooked. (About 20 minutes to the pound.) Remove the fish from the cooking liquor. Reserve 250 ml (½ pint) of the liquid for adding to the cream sauce.

Cut the turbot into flakes with a spoon, removing the bone and dark skin. The glutinous parts of the fish, including the meaty part of the fins, should be included as they are a great delicacy.

Mix the flaked fish into the cream sauce to make a stiffish consistency. Reserve extra sauce to serve separately. Stir the mixture over a low heat so that it is thoroughly heated through. Check the seasoning. Heap the fish into a shallow dome on an ovenproof dish. Fry the breadcrumbs lightly in the butter. Allow to cool slightly. Cover the fish 'thoroughly and smoothly' with the breadcrumbs and Parmesan cheese mixed together.

Pass a red-hot salamander over the breadcrumbed surface to melt the cheese and colour the dome of fish a golden brown. If you do not have a salamander place the dish in a very hot preheated oven for about 5 minutes. A little extra butter should be dotted over the surface in this case, to prevent the cheese and breadcrumb crust from drying out. Serve the fish immediately, surrounded by croquette potatoes or small crescents of puff pastry. Serve any remaining sauce in a sauceboat.

SERVES 4–6

✠

EDWARD VII

(1901–1910)

✢ ✢

EDWARD VII was once described as 'too human' for a king. He was not allowed by his mother to do anything worthwhile, so he dissipated his energies literally on wine, women and song. Yet when he finally became King at the age of sixty, he proved himself an excellent diplomatist and capable of inspiring great confidence and affection. When he visited Europe even the bones he left on his plate were sold as souvenirs. His successful reign only emphasizes what a waste his life had largely been until then.

Edward loved the good things of life and when he married Princess Alexandra of Denmark their home at Marlborough House became the centre of the fashionable world. The people who were part of their brilliant social circle were known as the Marlborough House Set. Alexandra herself was beautiful and sweet-natured with a charming daffiness. She could never manage to be on time for an appointment. At first Edward was devoted to her, but after a time his attentions began to wander to the other beauties of the day, women like Lady de Gray, Lady Dudley, Rachael Gurney and the 'Jersey Lily', Lily Langtry. It may partly have been because Alexandra grew increasingly deaf and cut off from what was going on that Edward started to leave her out of his social life. The frequent public scandals and Edward's unfaithfulness to his loyal wife turned many people against him for a long time. When an appendix operation forced him to postpone his coronation many clergymen considered it a divine warning that he should repent the error of his ways. Clearly Edward did not see things in the same light, for he was soon involved with yet another mistress, Mrs Keppel, to whom he remained devoted for the rest of his life. As he was dying, Alexandra, dignified and forgiving right until the end, allowed Mrs Keppel to come and spend some time with him.

As well as women, Edward loved horse racing, opera and music hall, and playing bridge. He also enjoyed travelling, and apart from frequent visits to the capital cities and spas of Europe he visited North America, Egypt and India. He thought he liked travelling incognito, but was invariably annoyed if he was not treated as a special person. Clothes were particularly important to him, especially uniforms, for he loved any sort of pomp and ceremony. He was infuriated if anyone wore a uniform incorrectly, or appeared inappropriately dressed for any occasion. When Lord Rosebery attended a dinner at Windsor Castle in evening clothes instead of dress uniform Edward did not allow the blunder to go unremarked but said icily to the offending guest, 'I see you belong to the American Embassy.' He was not often so unkind. At another dinner party he resorted to throwing asparagus stalks over his shoulder in order not to embarrass an Indian prince who had already started to do the same thing.

Treating his asparagus in such a contemptuous fashion cannot have been easy for a man who took his food so seriously that his friends nicknamed him 'Tum-Tum'. He was even superstitious on the subject and would get upset if two knives became crossed in front of him on the table. He would not sit down to a meal where the guests numbered thirteen, although he was once persuaded to do so because one of the guests, Princess Frederick Charles of Hesse, was pregnant. We know that Edward liked to eat grilled cutlets, baked potatoes with mayonnaise, oysters with brown bread and butter, *truite au bleue*, strawberries and *Nymphes à l'Aurore*. These last were frogs' legs in a champagne jelly which was garnished with fresh green herbs to look like a river. He drank champagne, preferably 1883 vintage, which was decanted into a glass jug. He invented a cocktail composed of whisky, Angostura bitters, maraschino, champagne, pineapple, lemon peel and sugar. He knew enough about food to devise several sauces and salad dressings as well. The habit of smoking after dinner was encouraged by him, and he himself smoked Corona y Corona cigars almost non-stop. When his love of food resulted in a girth which made it impossible for him to do up the lowest button on his waistcoat, his supremacy as a leader of fashion was such that other men assumed it was a new style and adopted it themselves.

Luckily for him, Edward's life of pleasure-seeking coincided with the careers of two men well qualified to supply his exacting culinary needs – the hotelier Ritz and the Master Chef Escoffier. These two men worked in partnership for years, creating the finest hotels in Europe and setting standards in luxury and food which have never been surpassed. Escoffier devised the system, used to this day in large kitchens, whereby different chefs make different components of the same dish rather than following one dish through from start to finish. He created many individual dishes for famous people. One of the best known is Peach Melba, made for the opera singer Dame Nellie Melba, a dear friend of Escoffier's. On the first occasion it was served it came to the table in a huge swan carved from a single block of ice. For Edward VII Escoffer created *Poularde Derby;* Edward was so impressed that afterwards he made a point of deliberately seeking out Escoffier's cooking whenever he was in Europe. This seal of royal approval guaranteed the fortunes of the two Frenchmen, for the fashionable set inevitably followed Edward's example. Some while later Ritz and Escoffier came to England to take over the Savoy and start the Ritz hotel. From then on Edward ate Escoffier's meals almost daily, in the company of fashionable friends like Ellen Terry, Beerbohm Tree and Sarah Bernhardt.

✣

POULARDE DERBY

The original recipe uses truffles, but as these are now so expensive I have substituted mushrooms.

*1 large chicken, 1.35–1.8 kg
  (3–4 lb)
salt
25 g (1 oz) melted butter
freshly ground black pepper*

*FOR THE MIREPOIX AND SAUCE:
450 g (1 lb) carrots, sliced
450 g (1 lb) onions, sliced
1 small head of celery
100 g (4 oz) lean bacon, minced
1 bay leaf
100 g (4 oz) butter
salt and freshly ground black
  pepper
250 ml (½ pint) light stock made
  with knuckle of veal
12 g (½ oz) arrowroot*

*FOR THE STUFFING:
100 g (4 oz) patna rice
50 g (2 oz) button mushrooms,
  diced
3 tablespoons double cream
75 g (3 oz) pâté de foie gras or
  similar smooth pâté, diced
salt, freshly ground black pepper*

*TO SERVE:
100 g (4 oz) button mushrooms
50 g (2 oz) pâté de foie gras or
  similar smooth pâté
25 g (1 oz) butter
croûtons*

Clean the chicken.

Prepare the mirepoix (vegetable base) by sweating the vegetables, bacon and bay leaf in the butter until soft. (About 15 minutes.) Season well. Line the bottom of a deep casserole with the mixture.

Prepare the stuffing by cooking the rice in boiling, salted water for about 9 minutes so that it is three quarters cooked. Drain the rice and combine it with the diced mushrooms, pâté and cream. Season very lightly. The rice will finish cooking inside the chicken and absorb the cream.

Stuff the chicken with the rice mixture. Place it in the casserole on the mirepoix, season well and brush with melted butter. Cover the dish and cook the chicken until tender in a moderate oven 180°C (350°F)/Gas 4. (About 1¾–2 hours.) Transfer the chicken to a hot serving dish and leave it to brown in the oven while you make the sauce.

To make the sauce add the veal stock to the vegetables left in the casserole and boil gently for about 10 minutes. Strain and pour off the grease. Mix the arrowroot with a little cold water and add it to the strained sauce. Reheat the sauce, stirring, until it thickens and the arrowroot clears. Adjust the seasoning.

Serve the chicken on a hot dish, surrounded by croûtons spread with pâté and whole button mushrooms, lightly cooked in butter. (The original recipe calls for whole truffles poached in champagne!) Serve the sauce separately.

SERVES 4

❖

This is a rich dish and is best served with a crisp green salad and perhaps a little plain boiled rice. Begin the meal with oysters, served with lemon juice and brown bread and butter, or consommé. As a dessert serve either *Peach Melba* made with homemade vanilla ice-cream, fresh peaches and real raspberry purée or *Pêches Alexandra*, for which Escoffier gives the following instructions.

Poach the peaches in a vanilla-flavoured syrup and let them cool completely. Dish them in a timbale surrounded by ice containing on its bottom a layer of vanilla ice-cream, covered with strawberry puree. Sprinkle the peaches with white and red rose petals, and veil the whole with spun sugar.

GENERAL INDEX

✢ ✢

155

RECIPE INDEX

✤ ✤